AF564403

National Higher Education Policy 2020

How to Make It Happen?

Khursheed Ahmad Butt

PUBLISHERS & DISTRIBUTORS (P) LTD

7/22, Ansari Road, Darya Ganj, New Delhi
Tel.: +91-11-4077 5252, 2327 3880
E-mail: orders@atlanticbooks.com
Web: www.atlanticbooks.com

This edition published in 2024 by Atlantic Publishers & Distributors (P) Ltd.

Printed & bound in India by Atlantic Print Services

Preface

Education is of paramount importance for the good of individuals, the society, the country, and the world. It develops qualified and professional human resources to manage the socio-economic reigns in a most efficient manner with a spirit of social justice, thus contributes to the socio-economic prosperity. It also enables nations to assume leadership at the global stage through the creation of new knowledge and cutting-edge technologies. Over and above, it acts as a great leveller by offering access to the unprivileged classes of the society to modern educational pursuits, thus promotes equity and justice in the society particularly where there exists huge gap between the rich and the poor, like our country.

The educational landscape world over has seen transformational changes with emergence of new knowledge domains like Artificial Intelligence, Big Data, Machine Learning, etc. These and other emerging knowledge domains are going to transform the working environs where there will be least intervention of human beings. The new knowledge economy will pave way for more skilled workforce. With climate change, increasing pollution, and depleting natural resources, there will be a sizeable shift in how we meet the world's energy, water, food, and sanitation needs, again resulting in the need for new skilled labour, particularly in biology, chemistry, physics, agriculture, climate science, and social science.

Our educational system though not being considered obsolete yet, it is not fully attuned to the changing world realities. The state of our higher education system becomes evident from the fact that none of the Indian universities figure among the first 100 and even among the top 300 global universities. The higher education system in India is beset with number of flaws and challenges particularly posed by the changing global landscape. The National Higher Educational Policy 2020 has identified a number of problems that are being currently confronted by the higher education in India, some of these problems include:

- a severely fragmented higher educational ecosystem with a rigid separation of disciplines, with early specialisation and streaming of students into narrow areas of study;
- limited teacher and institutional autonomy which hampers smooth functioning on sound lines of governance;
- limited access particularly in socio-economically disadvantaged areas, with few HEIs that teach in local languages;
- inadequate mechanisms for merit-based career management and progression of faculty and institutional leaders;
- lesser emphasis on research at most universities and colleges, and lack of competitive peer-reviewed research funding across disciplines;
- suboptimal governance and leadership of HEIs; and
- ineffective regulatory system and large affiliating universities resulting in low standards of undergraduate education.

NEP-2020 envisions a complete overhaul and re-energising of the higher education system to overcome these challenges with the purpose to deliver high-quality higher education, with improved equity and inclusion. The new policy offers far reaching amendments and transformational reforms in school and higher education. Apart from making students equipped with 21st century knowledge and skills, one of the stated aims of the policy is to instil pride in being Indian not only in thought but also in spirit, intellect, and deeds. The policy is founded on the five pillars of Equity and Access, Affordability, Quality, Creativity and Innovations, and Autonomy. It offers reforms towards reorganisation of regulatory systems, transformation of institutional structures, institutional autonomy, realignment of vocational education, teacher education, enabling learning environment, etc. The new policy offers some far reaching proposals which if implemented in letter and spirit will surely transform our higher education system.

Policies deliver due dividends only when implemented in letter and spirit. For effective implementation of this policy, at the top of everything it needs wholehearted support of the state governments as education is a state subject. At the institutional level, it needs strong commitment of vice chancellors and concerned state functionaries. But, ultimately effective planning in its implementation at the grass root level would be critical which among other things requires to have thorough debate and discussion among those who have to actually implement it both in letter and spirit. Timely infusion of requisite resources—human, infrastructural, and financial—at the Central and State levels will be crucial for the satisfactory execution of the policy. Besides, the policy contains some radical proposals like multidisciplinary education and Board of Governors for universities, but without any blueprint. It would serve a great purpose if centrally a complete blueprint for the implementation of these important proposals is prepared after debate and discussion. Periodical review of the implementation of the policy will be all the more important to align and realign proposals and processes if required.

This book is aimed to act as a guide to different stakeholders in the effective implementation of National Higher Education Policy 2020. Besides, it highlights certain question marks that exist in the new policy for further debate and discussion so that a fine tuning is done at the earliest so as to avoid any collateral damage. In line with these goals, the book has been organised into five sections. In the Section-I, the important proposals contained in the new policy have been highlighted so as enable the readers to understand their purpose and rationale. What needs to be done at different levels for the implementation of the various proposals in letter and spirit have been discussed in Section-II of the book. Besides, the question marks on some of the proposals have also been discussed in this section. On the most important aspect of higher education in India, i.e. Leadership and Governance, some meaningful proposals have been offered in the new policy, however, without detailed action plans. In the section-III, all the aspects of leadership and governance in higher educational institutions have been presented with full details. The discussion made in this section will go a long way to help the academic leaders in offering very effective and meaningful leadership and governance in their respective higher educational institutions. Last section of the book discusses the current state of the system of assessment and accreditation of higher education in the country and what needs to be done to make it more result oriented in the context of changing global realities. Here, an effort has been made to reframe Quality Indicator Framework (QIF) to make it more inclusive and objective with the sole purpose to make quality assessment very comprehensive with greater objectivity.

Some write-ups that have been published in local newspapers have been included in this book for wider circulation. Besides, the document of New Education Policy 2020 has been widely referred in this book.

Khursheed Ahmad Butt

Contents

Preface .... *iii*

Section One
Key Aspects of National Higher Education Policy 2020

1. Major Reformative Proposals of New Higher Education Policy 2020 Towards Institutional and Regulatory Framework 3

2. Understanding Multidisciplinary Education and other Proposals Contained in National Higher Education Policy 2020 10

3. Policy Proposals Towards Teacher Education in National Higher Education Policy 2020 18

4. Equity and Inclusion in National Higher Education Policy 2020 23

Section Two
Implementation of New Higher Education Policy

5. National Higher Education Policy 2020: How to Make it Happen? 31

6. Roadmap for the Implementation of Multidisciplinary Education System 37

7. Action Plan for the Implementation of Institutional and Faculty Autonomy Envisaged in National Higher Education Policy 2020 43

8. How to Integrate Vocational Education into Higher Education? 49

9. Faculty as Catalysts for Advances in Quality Teaching and Research 55

10. Internationalisation of Indian Education: Will it Arrest Brain Drain & Make India a Hub for International Students 61

11. Catalyzing Quality Research in Indian Universities 67

12. Whether Online Teaching-Learning Process and Evaluation is a Perfect Alternative to the Off-Line Mode? 73

Section Three
Leadership and Governance

13. Leadership Crisis in Indian Universities: Where the Rot Lies? 79

14. Appointment of Vice Chancellors in Indian Universities: Calls for a Procedural Rejig 85

15. Leadership Qualities of Successful Vice Chancellors in the Indian Context 92

16. Planning and Assessing Institutional Effectiveness: Panacea for all Ills in Higher Education in India 99

17. Evaluation of Teaching by Students: A Controversial Issue in Higher Education in India 106

18. Integrating Formative, Continuous and Comprehensive Assessment System into Higher Education 113

Section Four
Reforming Assessment and Accreditation Process

19. Quality Assurance in Indian Higher Education 121

20. Assessment and Accreditation of Higher Education: Calls for Refinements of Key Indicators of Quality Parameters 127

Quality Parameters 141

Index 173

SECTION ONE

Key Aspects of National Higher Education Policy 2020

- Major Reformative Proposals of New Higher Education Policy 2020 Towards Institutional and Regulatory Framework
- Understanding Multidisciplinary Education and other Proposals Contained in National Higher Education Policy 2020
- Policy Proposals Towards Teacher Education in National Higher Education Policy 2020
- Equity and Inclusion in National Higher Education Policy 2020

1

Major Reformative Proposals of New Higher Education Policy 2020 Towards Institutional and Regulatory Framework

Government of India announced National Education Policy 2020, replacing 34-year-old policy of 1986. The new policy offers major overhaul with important amendments and transformational reforms in school and higher education. Apart from making students equipped with 21st century knowledge and skills, one of the stated aims of the policy is to instil pride in being Indian not only in thought but also in spirit, intellect and deeds. The policy seems to have been founded on five pillars of Equity & Access; Affordability; Quality; Creativity & Innovations; and Greater Autonomy. With an aim to lay a strong and sound foundations for these five pillars, the new policy offers reforms towards reorganisation of regulatory systems, transformation of institutional structures, institutional autonomy, creation of multidisciplinary institutions, realignment of vocational education, teacher education, enabling learning environment with multidisciplinary education. In this chapter reforms undertaken in the regulatory and institutional set-up have been highlighted.

Graded Autonomy to Colleges and Universities

The most important takeaway of the new higher education policy is its emphasis on greater autonomy both at the institutional and faculty levels. In line with this direction, the new policy aims to upgrade the affiliating colleges into Autonomous Degree Granting Colleges by gradually phasing out the system of 'Affiliated Colleges' over a period of 15 years. Under the new policy, each existing affiliating university will be responsible for mentoring its affiliated colleges so that they can develop their capabilities and achieve minimum benchmarks in academic and curricular matters; teaching and assessment; governance; financial robustness; and administrative efficiency to become autonomous degree-granting colleges. Over a period of time, it is envisaged that every college would develop into either an autonomous degree-granting college, or a constituent college of a university. With appropriate accreditations, autonomous degree-granting colleges could evolve into Research-intensive or Teaching-intensive universities, if they so aspire.

With an aim to enable HEIs in effective governance, the new policy also offers a scope for universities to become independent self-governing institutions through a system of graded accreditation and graded autonomy, but in a phased manner over a period of 15 years. Upon receiving the appropriate graded accreditation, an university can become independent self-governing institution through the Board of Governors (BOG) consisting of a group of highly qualified, competent, and dedicated individuals, having proven capabilities and a strong sense of commitment to the institution. The BOG of an institution will be empowered to govern the institution free of any external interference, make all appointments including that of head of the institution, and take all decisions regarding governance. The BOG shall be responsible and accountable to the stakeholders through transparent self-disclosures of all relevant records. It will be also responsible for meeting all regulatory guidelines mandated by HECI through the National Higher Education Regulatory Council (NHERC).

Transformation of Institutional Structure

The other important policy recommendation of the new policy is structural transformation of HEIs aiming to make the focus of their goals and work crystal clear. Under the new policy, the HEIs have been structured into an 'University' and a 'College'. A university means a multidisciplinary institution of higher learning that offers undergraduate and graduate programmes. An university has been further classified into Research Intensive

Universities, and Teaching Intensive Universities. Research intensive universities shall be exclusively involved in high end research while as teaching intensive universities are mandated to have greater focus on teaching but can still conduct significant research. A college will refer to a large multidisciplinary institution of higher learning that is primarily focused on undergraduate teaching. The categorisation into three broad types of institutions are not in any natural way a rigid, exclusionary categorization, but HEIs will have the autonomy and freedom to move gradually from one category to another. Besides, the new policy recommends that the present complex nomenclature of HEIs in the country such as 'deemed to be university', 'affiliating university', 'affiliating technical university', 'unitary university' shall be replaced simply by 'University' on fulfilling the criteria as per norms.

Establishment of New National Research Foundation

India is confronted with number of challenges and problems like; pollution, poverty & inequality, regional imbalances, environmental degradation, etc. All these and other problems necessitate universities to conduct quality and actionable research. New policy recognises that a robust ecosystem of research is perhaps more important than ever with the rapid changes occurring in the world today, e.g., in the realm of climate change, population dynamics, biotechnology, an expanding digital marketplace, and the rise of machine learning and artificial intelligence. To grow and catalyze quality research in the nation, this policy envisions the establishment of a National Research Foundation (NRF) with the following primary activities:

- Fund competitive, peer-reviewed grant proposals of all types and across all disciplines;
- Seed, grow, and facilitate research at academic institutions, particularly at universities and colleges where research is currently in a nascent stage, through mentoring of such institutions;
- Act as a liaison between researchers and relevant branches of government as well as industry, so that research scholars are constantly made aware of the

most urgent national research issues, and also the policymakers are constantly made aware of the latest research breakthroughs; so as to allow breakthroughs to be optimally brought into policy and/or implementation; and

- Recognise outstanding research and progress.

Institutions that currently fund research, such as the Department of Science and Technology (DST), Department of Atomic Energy (DAE), Department of Bio-Technology (DBT), Indian Council of Agriculture Research (ICAR), Indian Council of Medical Research (ICMR), Indian Council of Historical Research (ICHR), as well as various private and philanthropic organizations, will continue to independently fund research according to their priorities and needs. However, NRF will carefully coordinate with other funding agencies to ensure synergy of purpose and avoid duplication of efforts.

Reorganisation of Regulatory System of Higher Education

Establishment of Higher Education Commission of India (HECI) with the subsequent winding up of UGC and AICTE has been a major step of the new policy to overcome the very basic problems with the existing regulatory system, such as; heavy concentration of power within a few bodies, conflicts of interest among these bodies, and a resulting lack of accountability. The HECI consists of four independent and empowered verticals (Bodies).

The first vertical will be the National Higher Education Regulatory Council (NHERC), empowered to regulate higher education excluding medical and legal education. It will regulate few important matters particularly Financial Probity, Good Governance, and the full online and offline public self-disclosure of all finances, audits, procedures, infrastructure, faculty/staff, and educational outcomes. Every institution shall be required to put in public domain the updated and accurate information relating to these matters on the website of NHERC and own institutional website. Any complaint or grievance from stakeholders and others arising out of the information placed in public domain shall be adjudicated by NHERC. Besides, feedback from randomly selected students including differently abled students will be solicited online to ensure valuable input at regular intervals.

The second vertical of HECI is National Accreditation Council (NAC). Accreditation of institutions will now be carried out by an independent ecosystem of 'Accrediting Institutions' supervised and overseen by NAC. The task to function as a recognized accreditor shall be awarded to an appropriate number of institutions by NAC. All HEIs will aim, through their Institutional Development Plans (IDPs), to attain the highest level of accreditation over the next 15 years to achieve the status of self-governing degree-granting institutions/clusters. In the long run, accreditation will become a binary process, as per the extant global practice.

The third vertical of HECI will be the Higher Education Grants Council (HEGC), which will carry out funding and financing of higher education based on transparent criteria, including the IDPs prepared by the institutions and the progress made on their implementation. HEGC will be entrusted with the disbursement of scholarships and developmental funds for launching new focus areas and expanding quality programme offerings at HEIs across disciplines and fields.

The fourth vertical of HECI will be the General Education Council (GEC), having a domain to set expected learning outcomes for higher education programmes, also referred to as 'graduate attributes.' A National Higher Education Qualification Framework (NHEQF) will be formulated by the GEC and it shall be in sync with the National Skills Qualifications Framework (NSQF) to ease the integration of vocational education into higher education. The GEC will be mandated to identify specific skills that students must acquire during their academic programmes, with the aim of preparing well-rounded learners with 21st century skills. In addition, the GEC shall set-up facilitative norms for issues, such as credit transfer, equivalence, etc., through the NHEQF.

The professional councils, such as the Indian Council for Agricultural Research (ICAR), Veterinary Council of India

(VCI), National Council for Teacher Education (NCTE), Council of Architecture (CoA), National Council for Vocational Education and Training (NCVET), etc., will act as Professional Standard Setting Bodies (PSSBs). They will play a key role in the higher education system and will be invited to be members of the GEC. The functioning of all the independent verticals for Regulation (NHERC), Accreditation (NAC), Funding (HEGC), and Academic Standard Setting (GEC) and the overarching autonomous umbrella body (HECI) itself will be based on transparent public disclosure, and use technology extensively to reduce human interface to ensure efficiency and transparency in their work. HECI itself will be resolving disputes among the four verticals.

Multidisciplinary Institutions

Towards achieving the goal of multidisciplinary education, the new policy offers moving towards a higher educational system consisting of large multidisciplinary universities and colleges. Accordingly, it aims at phasing out of the Single-stream HEIs over time to make such institutions multidisciplinary or parts of vibrant multidisciplinary HEI clusters. As per the new policy by 2040, all higher education institutions (HEIs) shall aim to become multidisciplinary institutions with larger student enrolments preferably in the thousands, however, initially should plan to become multidisciplinary by 2030, and then gradually increase student strength to the desired levels.

Internationalisation of Indian Higher Education

New policy also aims to make India as a hub for international students as well as provide greater mobility to Indian students who may wish to visit, study at, transfer credits to, or carry out research at institutions abroad, and vice versa. Towards the attainment of this goal, the policy offers the following policy recommendations:

- Offer Courses and programmes in subjects, such as Indology, Indian languages, AYUSH systems of medicine, yoga, arts, music, history, culture, and modern India. Courses in the sciences, social sciences, and beyond with internationally relevant curricula will also be offered to attract greater numbers of international students.

- HEI hosting foreign students will have to set-up an International Students Office to coordinate all matters relating to welcoming and supporting foreign students.
- Research/teaching collaborations and faculty/student exchanges with high-quality foreign institutions will be facilitated, and relevant mutually beneficial MOUs with foreign countries will be signed.
- High performing Indian universities will be encouraged to set-up campuses in other countries, and similarly, selected universities particularly those from among the top 100 universities in the world will be facilitated to operate in India. A legislative framework facilitating such entry will be put in place, and such universities will be given special dispensation regarding regulatory, governance, and content norms on par with other autonomous institutions of India.
- Research collaboration and student exchanges between Indian institutions and global institutions will be promoted through special efforts.
- Credits acquired in foreign universities will be permitted as per the requirements of each HEI, and counted for the award of a degree.

2

Understanding Multidisciplinary Education and other Proposals Contained in National Higher Education Policy 2020

National Education Policy 2020 offers sweeping changes in the regulatory systems, institutional structures, institutional autonomy, vocational education, teacher education, learning environment. In the previous chapter, reforms in the regulatory and institutional set-up have been highlighted. In this chapter, the other reforms initiated in higher education have been explained.

Making Undergraduate Education Multidisciplinary

To do away with a rigid separation of disciplines, with early specialisation and streaming of students into narrow areas of study, the new policy lays greater emphasis on multidisciplinary system of education. Students of arts and humanities will be required to learn more science subjects, similarly students belonging to science streams shall be required to learn subjects related to arts and humanities. Such an education is aimed to develop well-rounded individuals that possess critical 21st century capacities in fields across the arts, humanities, languages, sciences, social sciences, and professional, technical, and vocational fields. Even engineering institutions, such as IITs, will have to move towards multidisciplinary education with more arts and humanities subjects. In addition, the credit-based courses and projects in the areas of community engagement and service, environmental education, and value-based education shall have to be in the offing.

- Environment education will include areas like; climate change, pollution, waste management, sanitation, conservation of biological diversity, management of biological resources and biodiversity, forest and wildlife conservation, and sustainable development and living.

- Value-based education will include the development of humanistic, ethical, constitutional, and universal human values of truth (*satya*), righteous conduct (*dharma*), peace (*shanti*), love (*prem*), non-violence (*ahimsa*), scientific temper, citizenship values.
- Life-skills; lessons in *seva*/service and participation in community service programmes will be considered an integral part of a holistic education.

As part of a holistic education, the new policy also provides that the students at all HEIs will be provided with opportunities for internships with local industry, businesses, artists, craft persons, etc., as well as research internships with faculty and researchers of their own or other HEIs/research institutions, so that students may actively engage with the practical side of their learning and, as a by-product, further improve their employability.

Restructuring of UG/PG Degree Programmes

The restructuring of the existing 3-year undergraduate degree programme has been the other important policy recommendation. Under the new policy, the undergraduate degree programme will be of either 3 or 4-year duration, with multiple exit options, with appropriate certifications. If a student opts out after successfully completing 1st year, a certificate in a discipline or field including vocational and professional areas will be given, or a diploma after 2 years of study, or a bachelor's degree after a 3-year programme. The 4-year programme will lead to a degree 'with Research' if the student completes a rigorous research project in his or her major area(s) of study.

At the master's degree level, HEIs will have the flexibility to offer the following different duration/designs of master's programmes:

- 2-year programme with the second year devoted entirely to research for those who have completed the 3-year bachelor's programme;

- For the students who have a 4-year bachelor's programme with research, there could be a 1-year master's programme;
- Integrated 5-year bachelor's/master's programme;
- Undertaking a Ph.D. shall require either a master's degree or a 4-year bachelor's degree with Research. Ph.D. students shall have a minimum number of hours of actual teaching experience gathered through teaching assistantships and other means during their doctoral training period; and
- The M.Phil. programme has been discontinued.

Professional Education

Technical education includes degree and diploma programmes in, engineering, technology, management, architecture, town planning, pharmacy, hotel management, catering technology, etc., which are critical to India's overall development. There will not only be a greater demand for well-qualified manpower in these sectors, it will also require closer collaborations between industry and higher education institutions to drive innovation and research in these fields. Technical education will, thus, also aim to be offered within multidisciplinary education institutions and have a renewed focus on opportunities to engage deeply with other disciplines. India must also take the lead in preparing professionals in cutting-edge areas that are fast gaining prominence, such as Artificial Intelligence (AI), 3-D machining, big data analysis, and machine learning, in addition to genomic studies, biotechnology, nanotechnology, neuroscience, with important applications to health, environment, and sustainable living that will be woven into undergraduate education for enhancing the employability of the youth.

Realigning Vocational Education into Higher Education

On the lines of developed countries of the world, India also had emphasised on vocational education but has failed to achieve this cherished goal. The primary reasons cited for this dismal performance by the new policy include:

- Vocational education has in the past focused largely on Grades 11-12 and on dropouts in Grade 8 and upwards.
- Students passing out from Grades 11-12 with vocational subjects often did not have well-defined pathways to continue with their chosen vocations in higher education.
- The admission criteria for general higher education were also not designed to provide openings to students who had vocational education qualifications, leaving them at a disadvantage relative to their compatriots from 'mainstream' or 'academic' education.
- The vocational education is perceived to be inferior to mainstream education and meant largely for students who are unable to cope with the latter which to a great extent has affected the choices of students.

Given the above perceived bottlenecks, new policy aims to overcome the social status hierarchy associated with vocational education and offers integration of vocational education programmes into mainstream education. Beginning with vocational exposure at early ages in middle and secondary school, quality vocational education will be integrated smoothly into higher education. The policy aims that every child learns at least one vocation and is exposed to several more. Vocational education will be integrated in the educational offerings of all secondary schools in a phased manner over the next decade. Towards this, secondary schools will also collaborate with ITIs, polytechnics, local industry, etc. Skill labs will also be set up and created in the schools in a 'Hub and Spoke Model' which will allow other schools to use the facility.

Higher education institutions will offer vocational education either on their own or in partnership with industry and NGOs. The B.Voc. degrees will continue to exist, but vocational courses will also be available to students enrolled in all other bachelor's degree programmes, including the 4-year multidisciplinary bachelor's programmes. HEIs will also be allowed to conduct short-term certificate courses in various skills including soft skills. Focus areas for vocational education will be chosen based on skills gap analysis and mapping of local opportunities.

ODL and Online Education

To increase access to higher education, new policy also lays emphasis on Open Distance Learning (ODL) and online education. In order to leverage its potential completely, it is being envisioned in the new policy that ODL will be renewed through concerted, evidence-based efforts towards expansion while ensuring adherence to clearly articulated standards of quality. The policy document further states that ODL programmes will aim to be equivalent to the highest quality in-class programmes available. Norms, standards, and guidelines for systemic development, regulation, and accreditation of ODL will be prepared, and a framework for quality of ODL that will be recommendatory for all HEIs will be developed.

Creating Enabling Learning Environment

To ensure conducive environment for better learning outcomes, the new policy considers curriculum, pedagogy, continuous assessment, and student support as cornerstones for effective learning. As such, it recommends that the:

- Curriculum should be very much relevant, interesting and updated.
- Pedagogy used in the classroom should be engaging one in the sense that it should ensure active engagement of the learners rather being a one-sided affair.
- Assessment methods should aim to continuously improve learning. A continuous formative assessment system has been recommended to be used to further the goals of each programme.

To have most relevant and updated curriculum, engaging teaching pedagogy and the formative assessment system, the new policy offers institutional and faculty autonomy in these matters. Besides, requisite student support systems, such as quality libraries, classrooms, labs, technology, sports/recreation areas, etc. have been recognised by the new policy as equally important ingredients for enabling learning environment.

To achieve holistic development of students, each institution under the new policy would be required to create strong internal systems for supporting 'Diverse Student Cohorts' in academic and social domains both inside and outside formal academic classroom. The new policy requires that all HEIs will have mechanisms and opportunities for funding of topic-centred clubs and activities organized by students with the help of faculty and other experts as needed. Such clubs and events dedicated to science, mathematics, poetry, language, literature, debate, music, sports, etc.

Committed and Capable Faculty

Key to the achievement of greater excellence in higher education lies greatly in the committed and professionally qualified and capable faculty. Realising the centrality of the faculty, the new policy aims that the various factors that results into low faculty motivation levels must be addressed to ensure that each faculty member is committed towards advancing her/his students growth. Towards this end, the policy recommends that:

- All HEIs will be equipped with the basic infrastructural facilities.
- Teaching duties shall not be excessive, and student-teacher ratios not too high, so that there is adequate time for interaction with students, conducting research, and other university activities.
- Faculty will be appointed to individual institutions and generally not be transferable across institutions so that they feel truly invested in, connected to, and committed to their institution and community.
- Faculty will be given the freedom to design their own curricular and pedagogical approaches within the approved framework.
- Excellence will be further incentivized through appropriate rewards, promotions, recognitions, and movement into institutional leadership. Meanwhile, faculty not delivering on basic norms will be held accountable.
- The current recruitment process will be continued, however, a suitable probation period shall be put in place to further ensure excellence. There shall be a fast-track promotion system for recognizing high impact research and contribution.

- A system of multiple parameters for proper performance assessment, for the purposes of confirmation after probation, promotion, salary increases, recognitions, etc., shall be developed by each HEI which shall be clearly enunciated in it's Institutional Development Plan (IDP) which shall include peer and student reviews, innovations in teaching and pedagogy, quality and impact of research, professional development activities, and contribution to corporate social responsibility and the community.

Faculty Development

Professional development for college and university teachers will continue through the existing institutional arrangements and ongoing initiatives. However, these will be strengthened and substantially expanded to meet the needs of enriched teaching-learning processes for quality education. The use of technology platforms such as SWAYAM/DIKSHA for online training of teachers will be encouraged, so that standardized training programmes can be administered to large numbers of teachers within a short span of time. Towards achieving professional development of college and university teachers, the new policy recommends for the establishment of a National Mission for Mentoring, with a large pool of outstanding senior/retired faculty who would be willing to provide short and long-term mentoring/ professional support to university/college teachers.

Leadership and Governance

The presence of outstanding and enthusiastic institutional leaders that cultivate excellence and innovation is the need of the hour. Outstanding and effective institutional leadership is extremely important for the success of an institution and of its faculty. The new policy emphasizes that excellent faculty with high academic and service credentials as well as demonstrated leadership and management skills will be identified early and trained through a ladder of leadership positions. New policy requires that leadership positions shall not remain vacant, but rather an overlapping time period during transitions in leadership shall be the norm to ensure the smooth running of institutions. Institutional leaders will aim to create a culture of excellence that will motivate and incentivize outstanding and innovative teaching, research, institutional service, and community outreach from faculty members and all HEI leaders.

Equity and Access

To ensure greater equity and access, new policy lays emphasis to support successful transition to higher education to the students from socio-economically disadvantaged backgrounds. Universities and colleges will be encouraged and financially supported to set up high-quality support centres for this purpose. Financial assistance to students shall be made available through various measures. Efforts will be made to incentivize the merit of students belonging to SC, ST, OBC, and other SEDGs. As per the new policy in every education institution, there shall be counselling systems for handling stress and emotional adjustments.

GR Ratio

One of the important goals of the new policy is to increase the Gross Enrolment Ratio in higher education including vocational education from 26.3% in 2018 to 50% by 2035. The new policy emphasizes that while a number of new institutions may be developed to attain these goals, a large part of the capacity creation will be achieved by consolidating, substantially expanding, and also improving existing HEIs. Besides, to ensure full/easy access, equity and inclusion, more HEIs will be established in underserved regions of the country. There shall, by 2030, be at least one large multidisciplinary HEI in or near every district.

Public Expenditure on Education

In order to attain the goal of education with excellence and the corresponding multitude of benefits to this Nation and its economy, this policy unequivocally endorses and envisions a substantial increase in public investment in education by both the Central Government and all State Governments. The policy proposes that Centre and the States shall work together to increase the public investment in education sector to reach 6% of GDP at the earliest. This is considered extremely critical for achieving high-quality and equitable public education system that is truly needed for India's future economic, social, cultural, intellectual, and technological progress and growth.

3

Policy Proposals Towards Teacher Education in National Higher Education Policy 2020

Teacher is central to the education at all levels be it; school education, higher education, professional education. A teacher need not to have only subject knowledge, but to be successful, he or she also need to possess many other personality traits which can be developed through an exposure to teacher education and trainings. Teaching at higher education level is somewhat not that intricate or difficult task than at a school level. A school teachers is required to mould children who need to be handled in a careful manner as being very delicate young souls. In view of this fact, the teacher education has evolved as a distinct subject with an aim to train and develop teachers with requisite expertise. Teacher education is an educational programme, in India generally offered by universities or specialised teacher education institutes, with a goal to develop teacher proficiency and competence that would enable teachers to teach in a most efficient manner. According to the International Encyclopaedia of teaching and teacher education (1987), "Teacher education can be considered in three phases, viz., Pre-service, Induction and In-service. The three phases are considered as three parts of a continuous process."

In India, the policy planners did emphasise on teacher education to ensure qualified and competent teachers who possess teaching skills, pedagogical approaches and professional skills. Post-independence, Government of India took the task of building the system of teacher education on the modern lines. Many committees and commissions were constituted to recommend measures to be taken to strengthen the teacher education at all levels. The most important committees and commissions include; University Education Commission, Secondary Education Commission, National Policy Statement on Education, National Commission on Teachers-I, National Policy of Education, Yashpal Committee, National Curriculum Framework, National Knowledge Commission and National Curriculum Framework for Teacher Education. Consequent upon the recommendations of these and other commissions and committees, there have been significant developments towards teacher education at all levels of education in thè country which certainly have contributed to the growth and development of our systems of education. Currently, an elaborate systems for Pre-service, Induction and In-service training are available for all sorts of teachers in the country. But there are serious question marks on the quality of teaching and training that is being currently offered by the various institutions created for the purpose. The poor quality of education and training offered by various teacher education institutes is being viewed as a major challenge to the entire system of education in the country.

New Education policy acknowledges the utter failure of teacher education in the country. Citing the Justice Verma Commission Report, the new policy states that the stand-alone Teacher Education Institutions (TEIs) are not attempting serious teacher education but are essentially selling degrees for a price, putting blame for such a failure squarely on regulatory mechanism for having failed to enforce basic standards for quality. Given such a sad state affairs, the new policy argues that the sector and its regulatory systems are in urgent need of revitalization through radical action, in order to raise standards and restore integrity, credibility, efficacy, and high quality in the teacher education system. Towards ensuring quality teacher education, the new policy offers following policy recommendations:

- The regulatory system shall be empowered to take stringent action against substandard and dysfunctional teacher education institutions (TEIs) that do not meet basic educational criteria, after giving one year for remedy of the breaches.

- All teacher education programmes must be conducted within composite multidisciplinary institutions. To this end, all multidisciplinary universities and colleges will aim to establish education departments which, besides carrying out cutting-edge research in various aspects of education, will also run B.Ed. programmes, in collaboration with other departments such as psychology, philosophy, sociology, neuroscience, Indian languages, arts, music, history, literature, physical education, science and mathematics.
- All stand-alone TEIs shall be required to convert to multidisciplinary institutions by 2030, so as to enable such institutions to offer the 4-year integrated teacher preparation programme. The 4-year integrated B.Ed. programme to be offered by such multidisciplinary HEIs will, by 2030, become the minimal degree qualification for school teachers.
- The 4-year integrated B.Ed. will be a dual-major holistic bachelor's degree, in Education as well as a degree with a specialized subject such as, a language, history, music, mathematics, computer science, chemistry, economics, arts, physical education, etc.
- The HEIs offering the 4-year integrated B.Ed. may also run a 2-year B.Ed., for students who have already received a bachelor's degree in a specialized subject. The new policy also allows to offer a 1-year B.Ed. to the candidates who have received a 4-year undergraduate degree in a specialized subject.
- Scholarships for meritorious students will be established for the purpose of attracting outstanding candidates to the 4-year, 2-year, and 1-year B.Ed. programmes.
- Each higher education institution will have a network of government and private schools to work closely with, where potential teachers will have the opportunity to teach along with participating in other activities such as community service, adult and vocational education, etc.

- In order to maintain uniform standards for teacher education, the admission to pre-service teacher preparation programmes shall be through suitable subject and aptitude tests conducted by the National Testing Agency, and shall be standardized keeping in view the linguistic and cultural diversity of the country.
- All fresh Ph.D. entrants, irrespective of discipline, will be required to take credit-based courses in teaching/education/pedagogy/writing related to their chosen Ph.D. subject during their doctoral training period. Ph.D. students will also have a minimum number of hours of actual teaching experience gathered through teaching assistantships and other means.

All the above measures if implemented in letter and spirit will go a long way in improving the teacher education in the country. But the perennial problem with which our education has been confronted is that the teaching as a career has been the last resort for our youth. Though, to attract the meritorious students to the 4-year, 2-year, and 1-year B.Ed. programmes, the new policy offers a provision of scholarships to the outstanding candidates, but it is unlikely to serve the purpose. Something more radical needs to be done to attract the outstanding candidates towards the profession of teaching. Offering very lucrative pay packages to the school teachers with a status of 'Special Citizens' would be needed to change the perception of our young generation towards this great profession. Besides, making regulatory system to work with all the seriousness required to ensure quality teacher education by the Teacher Education Institutes (TEIs) would be all the more important. Lack of powers with the regulators to ensure quality education is not viewed as the cause for poor quality but the lack seriousness on the part of the regulators to exercise powers to take stringent action against the dysfunctional teacher education institutions has been the main problem. Therefore, it is good to give more powers to the regulators to ensure standard quality but equally important would be to take all the necessary steps to ensure that the regulator acts and acts more enthusiastically to take stringent action against the erring institutions.

It is also that the new policy has offered nothing towards the UGC sponsored Academic Staff Colleges which are involved in the training and development of college and university teachers. These colleges mainly conduct orientation/induction programmes of newly recruited teachers and subject-wise refresher courses to refresh teachers about the latest developments happening in their respective subjects. UGC periodically assess these colleges but no worthwhile study by the third party has been conducted so far to assess the success of these colleges. These colleges conduct regularly various training programmes but it is not clear how far these have succeeded to achieve the intended outcomes of the various programmes. There are clear indications that the role performance of these colleges have been far from satisfactory for the reasons of their greater focus on the achievement of the targets in terms of number of programmes conducted rather than making serious attempts to achieve the intended goals of different programmes. The more appropriate would be that there are well-defined measurable intended outcomes for each programme of these colleges and at the end of each year there is a third-party evaluation organised and supervised by the funding agency. Besides, the funding should be linked to the success in achieving the intended outcomes of the programmes conducted by the colleges rather merely on the basis of the number of training programmes conducted.

Among other things, the most important takeaway of the policy recommendation towards teachers education has been that all fresh Ph.D. entrants, irrespective of discipline, will be required to take credit-based courses in teaching/education/pedagogy/ writing related to their chosen Ph.D. subject during their doctoral training period. Apart from gaining thorough knowledge of the subject and research methods, the scholars will gain much useful experience of teaching which ultimately, they will have to practice. However, the success of this policy initiative will depend upon how seriously the research supervisors will plan and execute teaching assignments of their registered scholars.

4

Equity and Inclusion in National Higher Education Policy 2020

India is the second most populous country in the world with nearly one fifth of the world's population. According to the 2019 revision of the World Population Prospects, the population of India stood at 1,352,642,280 persons. India is projected to surpass China to become the world's most populous country by 2024. It is expected to become the first country to be home to more than 1.5 billion people by 2030, and its population is set to reach 1.7 billion by 2050. Its population growth rate is 1.13%, ranking 112th in the world in 2017. India has more than 50% of its population below the age of 25 and more than 65% below the age of 35 which promises huge potential for economic growth and development. It is expected that, in 2020, the average age of an Indian will be 29 years, compared to 37 for China and 48 for Japan; and, by 2030, India's dependency ratio should be just over 0.4.

Apart from being the second most populous country in the world, India is also a home to the world's most poor people. But the pleasing aspect is that the poverty in India is on decline after witnessing a sustained economic growth during the last few decades, with close to 18 Indians escaping extreme poverty every minute, as per the World Poverty Clock. India has 86.8 million people living in extreme poverty which makes up 6% of its total population as of early 2021. In May 2012, the World Bank reviewed and proposed revisions to their poverty calculation methodology by adopting purchasing power parity basis method for measuring poverty worldwide. As of 2020, the incidence of multidimensional poverty has significantly reduced from 54.7 per cent in 2005 to 27.9 per cent in 2015-16. According to United Nations Development Programme Administrator Achim Steiner, India lifted 21 million people out of poverty in a 10-year time period from 2005-06 to 2015-16.

"Ending poverty in all its forms everywhere" is the first of the 17 sustainable development goals set by the United Nations with a pledge that no one will be left behind. Economic growth is considered as one of the principal instruments for poverty alleviation and for pulling the poor out of poverty through productive employment. Studies from Africa, Brazil, China, Costa Rica, and Indonesia have shown that rapid economic growth lifted a significant number of poor people out of financial poverty between 1970 and 2000. Apart from having a greater focus on economic growth and development as a means to alleviate poverty, different governments in India have employed multiple strategies towards poverty alleviation which includes creating financial and social safety nets. Combined with the number of social safety net programmes and public spending on social protection, in India the policy of reservations in government jobs and for admission in educational institutions to the applicants belonging to the Socially and Economically Disadvantaged Groups (SEDGs) have been used as a means to alleviate poverty. It is an established fact that education acts as a great leveller between the rich and poor. In the past, there have been reservations in educational institutions only for the students belonging to the socially disadvantaged groups of the society. But realising the fact that the poor people also exists in other classes of the society, therefore, in 2018, Government of India created a provision for 10 per cent reservation in educational institutions for the students belonging to the economically poorer sections of the society which really was need of the hour. Though the policy of reservations continued since long, but there is a realisation that this policy has to continue till the last person is taken out of poverty.

There is an explicit emphasis in new education policy on ensuring greater access to education particularly to the students belonging to the SEDGs. The new education policy is of the opinion that the reasons for exclusion of the students belonging to the SEDGs from the education system are common across school and higher education sectors. Therefore, the approach to equity and inclusion must be common across school and higher education. As per the new policy there are certain facets of exclusion, that are particular to or substantially more intense in higher education which include lack of knowledge of higher education opportunities, economic opportunity, cost of pursuing higher education, financial constraints, admission processes, geographical and language barriers, poor employability, potential of many higher education programmes, and lack of appropriate student support mechanisms. In view of these reasons, the new policy lays much emphasis to overcome these constraints so that there is greater access to educational pursuits to the students belonging to the SEDGs.

Towards the goal of achieving greater equity and inclusion, NEP-2020 makes wide ranging recommendations in the policy document. The far-reaching recommendations include the steps to be taken at the governmental level and at the Higher Educational level:

Steps to be taken by Governments

- Earmark suitable government funds for the education of SEDGs
- Set clear targets for higher GER for SEDGs
- Enhance gender balance in admissions in HEIs
- Enhance access by establishing more high-quality HEIs in aspirational districts and Special Education Zones containing larger numbers of SEDGs
- Develop and support high-quality HEIs that teach in local/Indian languages or bilingually
- Provide more financial assistance and scholarships to the students belonging to the SEDGs in both public and private HEIs
- Conduct outreach programmes on higher education opportunities and scholarships among SEDGs

- Develop and support technology tools for better participation and learning outcomes.

Steps to be taken at Higher Educational Levels

- Mitigate opportunity costs and fees for pursuing higher education
- Provide more financial assistance and scholarships to socio-economically disadvantaged students
- Conduct outreach programmes for the students belonging to SEDGs on higher education opportunities and scholarships
- Make admissions processes more inclusive for the students belonging to SEDGs.
- Make curriculum more inclusive
- Increase employability potential of higher education programmes
- Develop more degree courses taught in Indian languages and bilingually
- Ensure all buildings and facilities are wheelchair-accessible and disabled-friendly
- Develop bridge courses for students that come from for SEDGs
- Provide socio-emotional and academic support and mentoring for the students belonging to SEDGs through suitable counselling and mentoring programmes
- Ensure sensitization of faculty, counsellors, and students on gender-identity issue and its inclusion in all aspects of the HEI, including curricula
- Strictly enforce all no-discrimination and anti-harassment rules
- Develop Institutional Development Plans that contain specific plans for action on increasing participation from SEDGs.

The steps enumerated above are very comprehensive, thus if implemented with vigour and enthusiasm, are sure to help to achieve greater equity and access in higher education in the country. Steps at the government level like; to earmark suitable funds for the education of SEDGs, to enhance access by establishing more high-quality HEIs in aspirational districts and Special Education Zones containing larger numbers of SEDGs and to develop and support high-quality HEIs that teach in local/ Indian languages or bilingually, are very significant steps towards achieving greater equity and access to the students belonging to SEDGs. However, it will be seen whether the state governments will be able to earmark more funds for the education of SEDGs. Besides, it is being argued that it is not a progressive proposal to emphasise on the mother tongue as a medium of instruction when English language is widely associated with employability and privilege in the country. Developing bridge courses for the students that come from disadvantaged and educationally backgrounds groups of the society would be more appropriate to help them to catch up with the other groups of students which in turn will enable them to compete well in the job markets.

It is a most welcome step to declare special education zones where there is a large population belonging to SEDGs. This will enable the governments to have a greater focus in these areas by implementing all the schemes and programmes. However, in school education, there is a problem of lack of requisite infrastructural facilities in the schools located in the rural areas. Unless and until, the lack of infrastructural facilities in rural schools is taken care-off, the new policy is unlikely to achieve much. This would require to make huge investments, which given the state of finances of the governments, it is not likely to see much improvement in the infrastructural index of rural schools. Besides, there exists a huge gap in the quality of education in government run schools and private English medium schools located in cities and urban areas which to a great extent determines the competitiveness of their students. The students belonging to the government run schools are largely constrained in terms of quality education while as the students of private English medium schools enjoy access to quality educational pursuits. It is, therefore, due to this mismatch in the quality of education offered in these two types of schools that the wards belonging to SEDGs end up losing while competing with the students belonging to the English medium schools. To bridge the gap between the rich and poor through the medium of education, there is an urgent need to ensure that the students of government run schools enjoy access to the same quality of education as is available to the students in premium English medium schools. Therefore, it was expected from the policy makers to take some 'Out of Box' measures so that the students of government run schools who mainly belong to SEDGs enjoys access to same quality education as is being enjoyed by the students belonging to the economically affluent classes.

SECTION TWO

Implementation of New Higher Education Policy

- National Higher Education Policy 2020: How to Make it Happen?
- Roadmap for the Implementation of Multidisciplinary Education System
- Action Plan for the Implementation of Institutional and Faculty Autonomy Envisaged in National Higher Education Policy 2020
- How to Integrate Vocational Education into Higher Education?
- Faculty as Catalysts for Advances in Quality Teaching and Research
- Internationalisation of Indian Education: Will it Arrest Brain Drain & Make India a Hub for International Students?
- Catalyzing Quality Research in Indian Universities
- Whether Online Teaching-Learning Process and Evaluation is a Perfect Alternative to the Off-Line Mode?

5

National Higher Education Policy 2020: How to Make it Happen?

Government of India announced new education policy in July 2020 which replaces a 34-year-old policy of 1986. The new policy is being projected by the government as a significant milestone in the history of Indian education. The importance of this policy to the union government becomes evident from the fact that the Prime Minister has personally spoken in detail number of occasions about the significance of this policy. Many educationists have hailed this policy as a path-breaking and progressive, offering many transformational reforms both in school and higher education system. But there are others who have some serious reservations regarding some of the proposals contained in the new policy. It is being argued that it is not a progressive proposal to emphasise on the mother tongue as a medium of instruction when English language is widely associated with employability and privilege in the country. An article in *ThePrint* has articulated very eloquently how having proficiency in English language has contributed to the economic prosperity of our nation. There is no denying the fact that there are some question marks about the utility of some of the proposals but overall, this policy contains many useful proposals. With respect to higher education, the new policy contains many useful proposals which if implemented in letter and spirit, have the potential to take higher education to greater heights. Some of the important takeaways of NEP-2020 for higher education includes:

- Transformation of discipline centric into a multidisciplinary system of education to develop well-rounded individuals, possessing critical 21st century capacities in fields across the arts, humanities, languages, sciences, social sciences, professional, and vocational fields.
- Creation of Academic Credit Bank (ACB) to facilitate transfer of credits between different HEIs is the other notable feature of NEP-2020. The new policy also allows students an option of a sabbatical leave to re-join after some time to complete the degree without losing credits already earned.
- Creation of strong internal systems for supporting 'Diverse Student Cohorts' in academic and social domains both inside and outside formal academic classroom is another useful proposal of the policy. It would be essential for HEIs to have mechanisms and opportunities for funding of topic-centred clubs and activities organized by students with the help of faculty and other experts.
- Allows faculty to be appointed to individual institutions and generally not be transferable across institutions so that they feel truly invested in, and committed to their institution and community.
- Requires excellence to be incentivized through appropriate rewards, promotions, recognitions, and movement into institutional leadership. There shall be a fast-track promotion system for recognizing high impact research.
- Each HEI shall develop a system of multiple parameters for performance assessment for the purposes of confirmation, promotion, salary increases, recognitions, etc., which shall be clearly enunciated in Institutional Development Plan (IDP).
- To ensure greater equity and access, new policy lays emphasis to support successful transition to higher education to the students with socially and economically disadvantaged backgrounds. Universities and colleges will be encouraged and financially supported to set up high-quality support centres for this purpose.

- Greater autonomy both at the institutional and faculty levels is envisaged in the policy. In line with this goal, the new policy aims to upgrade the affiliating colleges into Autonomous Degree Granting Colleges by gradually phasing out the system of 'Affiliated Colleges' over a period of 15 years.
- Provides for universities to become self-governing institutions through a system of graded accreditation and graded autonomy, but in a phased manner over a period of 15 years. Upon receiving the appropriate graded accreditations, a university can become independent self-governing institution through the Board of Governors (BoG).
- The present complex nomenclature of HEIs in the country such as 'deemed to be university', 'affiliating university', 'affiliating technical university', 'unitary university' has been done away and now there will be a nomenclature of a university or college only.
- To make the focus of their goals and work crystal clear, HEIs have been structured into a 'University' and a 'College'. A university can be a 'Research Intensive', or a 'Teaching Intensive'. A College will refer to a large multidisciplinary institution that is primarily focused on undergraduate teaching.
- New policy recognises that a robust ecosystem for research is perhaps more important than ever with the rapid changes taking place in the world today in the realm of climate change, biotechnology, digital marketplace, and the rise of machine learning and artificial intelligence. Therefore, to grow and catalyze quality research in HEIs, the new policy proposes the establishment of a National Research Foundation (NRF).
- Establishment of Higher Education Commission of India (HECI) has been a major step of the new policy to overcome the very basic problems with the existing regulatory system, such as; heavy concentration of power within a few bodies, conflict of interests, and lack of accountability. The HECI

shall consist of four independent and empowered verticals, viz., NHERC, NAC, HEGC and GEC.

- Towards achieving the goal of multidisciplinary education, the new policy offers moving towards a higher educational system consisting of large multidisciplinary universities and colleges. Accordingly, it aims at phasing out of the Single-stream HEIs over time to make such institutions multidisciplinary or parts of vibrant multidisciplinary HEI clusters.
- New policy also aims to make India as a hub for international students as well as provide greater mobility to Indian students who may wish to study at, transfer credits to, or carry out research abroad, and vice versa. High performing Indian universities will be encouraged to set up campuses in other countries, and similarly, universities particularly those from among the top 100 global universities will be facilitated to operate in India.
- Targets to increase Grass Enrolment Ratio in higher education including vocational education from current 26.3% to 50% by 2035.
- Establishment of model Public universities for holistic and multidisciplinary education, at par with IITs, IIMs, etc., called MERUs also emphasised in the new policy.
- HEIs shall move away from the current semester-end summative examination towards continuous and comprehensive formative evaluation is being recommended in the policy.
- Vocational education will be integrated into the system of education and by 2025, at least 50% of the learners through school and higher education system shall have exposure to vocational education.

There are some proposals which are quite challenging thus, difficult to implement and some other proposals instead of doing any good, are likely to prove counterproductive. The 4-year programme is recommended to lead to a degree with 'Research' if students complete a rigorous research project in his or her major area(s) of study. However, a 4-year programme leading to degree with 'Research' is unlikely to serve a meaningful purpose as it would be a daunting job for HEIs to ensure quality of research for obvious reasons. Similarly, 2-year master's programme with second year devoted entirely to research for those who have completed 3-year bachelor's programme would do no good rather such a move will only deteriorate its quality. It is also that the provision of admission to Ph.D. programme with bachelor's degree would be unfeasible, rather unwise move because such students have not yet mastered the subject in which he or she will pursue research. Besides, doing away with the system of affiliating colleges by upgrading the existing affiliated college into an 'Autonomous Degree Granting Colleges' (ADGCs) is likely to serve little or no purpose for two reasons, One, that granting academic autonomy without administrative autonomy would be meaningless. Second, this concept of ADGCs has been in vogue but has been found to have done no good to the academics in the colleges which have been granted such a status. Establishment of NRF most likely would end up to the extent of an addition of one more institution, funding peer-reviewed grant proposals. It is good to try to address the problem of the lack of sufficient funding but it was equally important to address the other issues inhibiting the conduct of quality research of international standards in Indian universities.

Politicians and many academicians have exhibited exuberance and confidence that the steps taken in the NEP-2020 will not only make India as a hub for international students but will stop Indian students going abroad as the world class educational opportunities will be available right here, once top 100 global universities will set-up campuses in India. The exuberance shown by the government functionaries and others about the potential of NEP-2020 to make India as a hub for the international students and in putting a break on 'Brain Drain' by stopping Indian students going abroad, realistically speaking, it is more in "Rhetoric Than in Reality." A strong push by the government and the HEIs will help in getting international students but not in large numbers and that too generally from Africa and some South Asian countries. The reason being that it is not only in the search for world class education, Indian students go abroad but more for an opportunity to settle in the western world for the reasons of having access to the promising professional prospects and better quality of life.

These are justifiable question marks but overall the policy has to offer a lot to the higher education system provided implemented successfully. Policies deliver due dividends only when implemented in letter and spirit. For effective implementation of this policy, at the top of everything it needs wholehearted support of the state governments as education is a state subject. At the HEI level, it needs strong commitment of the Vice Chancellors and concerned state functionaries. But ultimately effective planning in its implementation at the gross root level would be critical which among other things would need to have thorough debate and discussion among those who have to actually implement it both in letter and spirit. Timely infusion of requisite resources—human, infrastructural, and financial—at the Central and State levels will be crucial for the satisfactory execution of the policy. Besides, the policy contains some radical proposals like multidisciplinary education, Board of Governors for universities but without any blueprint. It would serve a great purpose if centrally a complete blueprint for the implementation of these important proposals are prepared after debate and discussion. Periodical review of the implementation of the policy will be all the more important to align and realign proposals and processes if required.

The policy has enunciated the following principles for its implementation. First, implementation of the spirit and intent of the policy will be the most critical matter. Second, it is important to implement the policy initiatives in a phased manner, as each policy point has several steps, each of which requires the previous step to be implemented successfully. Third, prioritization will be important in ensuring optimal sequencing of policy points, and that the most critical and urgent actions are taken up first, thereby enabling a strong base. Fourth, comprehensiveness in implementation will be key; as this policy is interconnected and holistic, only a full-fledged implementation, and not a piecemeal one, will ensure that the desired objectives are achieved. Finally, careful analysis and review of the linkages between multiple parallel implementation steps will be necessary in order to ensure effective dovetailing of all initiatives.

6

Roadmap for the Implementation of Multidisciplinary Education System

In real life situations, a graduate would require not only to have a thorough understanding of the knowledge required to discharge professional duties in a most effective manner, but also of the entire ecosystem of political, social, legal, historical, cultural, and technological. Therefore, the graduates coming out of universities need to have a holistic understanding of the world around them which in turn calls for multidisciplinary approach to education. In developed parts of the world, higher education is multidisciplinary which exposes students to diverse disciplines, thoughts, perspectives and skill sets. Exposure to diverse disciplines enables one to amalgamate different perspectives of the subject matter, leading into a wholesome personality. But currently higher education offerings in India are fragmented into silos, as a result fails to produce well rounded graduates thus, unable to see the world around them with all the required lenses. This discipline-centered education fails to develop the overall personality of a student, i.e. his/her intellectual, aesthetic, social, physical, emotional, and moral attributes of a personality in an integrated manner.

To deliver high-quality higher education with equity and inclusion, the new policy envisions a complete overhaul and re-energising of the higher education system to overcome the challenges and problems being faced by HEIs. One of the problems reported by the new policy being currently faced by the higher education system in India is, a rigid separation of disciplines, with early specialisation and streaming of students into narrow areas of study. To do away with this problem, the new policy lays greater emphasis on multidisciplinary system of education. Such an education is aimed to develop well-rounded individuals possessing critical 21st century capacities in fields across the arts, humanities, languages, sciences, social sciences, professional, and vocational fields. Even the engineering institutions, such as IITs, will have to move towards multidisciplinary education with more arts and humanities subjects.

Introduction of multidisciplinary education at undergraduate level is one of the important features of the NEP-2020. But the policy document only makes a mere mention of this new system without any detailed blueprint which is essential for its implementation in letter and spirit. It merely talks about moving towards a higher educational system consisting of large, multidisciplinary universities and colleges, with at least one in or near every district. Besides, it aims at phasing out of the Single-stream HEIs over time. To standardise the implementation of multidisciplinary education, at least it was needed to draw a broad sketch of this new system to be put in place in the policy. While implementing multidisciplinary system of education, most important step would be to design a broad format of the course structure to be followed. Based on the experiences of different models of multidisciplinary educational structures in vogue in different parts of the world, the structure consisting of the courses classified into; College Core, Discipline Core, and Subject Core would be most appropriate to follow.

- **College Core:** It include a series of courses that the students across all streams shall have to learn as being essential ingredients of a wholesome personality. These courses generally are aimed to harness critical thinking, logic and analysis; mathematics and quantitative reasoning; communication skills, and sound grounding in social sciences, humanities, management, civics, creative arts and sciences. It generally includes courses on languages both written and spoken, literature, history, civics, political science, mathematics, information communication technology, philosophy, sociology, psychology, creative arts, public health, conservation, organisational behaviour, management, Indian economy, and entrepreneurship.

- **Discipline Core:** The discipline refers to a branch of academic study having varied functional areas like sciences, humanities, social sciences, law, commerce and management. Therefore, discipline core includes the courses that are compulsorily to be learned by the students of a particular discipline regardless of their areas of specialisation. It is not necessary that all disciplines will have same number of core courses, rather would vary depending upon the nature of each discipline. The core courses of different disciplines are generally well defined, however, additions and deletions take place with the changing phenomenon of the discipline.
- **Subject Core:** Subject in academics refers to a specific or specialised branch of knowledge of a discipline. The courses which are specifically related to a specific speciality, are referred to as subject core. These vary from subject to subject and are necessary to learn to gain a specialised knowledge and skill sets of a specialised branch.

How many credit hours required to graduate in a given discipline/subject are not mentioned in the policy document. Typically, in order to graduate with bachelor's degree, students are expected to complete 120-140 credit hours, every year 30-40 credits. Generally, science streams requires 140 credits and all other streams 120 credits. The credit hour should vary between 3-4 hours for each course. For all those courses, where lab work is involved, such courses typically carry 4 credit hours and all other courses are assigned 3 credits only. Besides, a 4-year bachelor's degree programme, the minimum number of credits should be 150-170. For master's degree, generally, a student is required to earn 80-90 credits. Given the universal practices, the break-up of the total credits for bachelor's degree should be 36 credits for college core, 54 credits for discipline core and 30 credits for subject core which would include option of internship or research project of 9-10 credits.

The other issue concerning the implementation of Choice Based Multidisciplinary Education is that, "Should certain number of selected courses be offered per semester or should the students have the freedom to choose the courses for each semester within the framework of maximum and minimum course ceilings, and course prerequisites. Given the spirit of choice-based credit system, the choice to select the courses in a particular semester should lie with the students, therefore, it would be appropriate to only identify the total number of courses for each group, viz., College Core, Discipline Core and Subject Core and allow freedom to the students to choose the courses for each semester. This will allow the students to complete the degree at their convenient pace. Also, there should be a freedom to the students to take a sabbatical leave and come back to complete the degree with a well-defined shelf life for the credits already earned, which has been envisioned in the new policy as well. The fact is that the CBCS in vogue in the colleges in Kashmir is not truly a choice-based system. It offers only one choice to choose general electives from a basket of electives but denies students an opportunity to plan the completion of their degrees at their own pace, facility of credit transfers and freedom to take a sabbatical leave to re-join after some time to complete degree without losing the credits already earned, thus in contravention to the true spirit of CBCS.

Under the new policy, the undergraduate programme will be of either 3 or 4-year duration, with multiple exit options, and with appropriate certifications. After 1st year, a certificate in a discipline or a field including vocational, or a diploma after 2 years of study, or a bachelor's degree after a 3-year programme would be awarded. The 4-year programme will also be in the offing leading to a degree with 'Research' if the student completes a rigorous research project in his or her major area(s) of study. Allowing multiple exit options with appropriate certifications and also an option of a sabbatical leave to re-join to complete the degree would offer greater flexibility to the students to pursue their studies. However, 4-year programme leading to degree with 'Research' is likely to serve no meaningful purpose for the reasons that the students:

- Pursuing still bachelor's degree are not yet qualified and capable to undertake any meaningful research;

- Are not yet well equipped with the tools and techniques of research;
- Are yet to gain mastery in the subject of his specialisation;
- Largeness of students and lack of qualified faculty who are already suffering from excessive workload would render the proposal of little or no use.

In view of the above constraints, the option of bachelor's degree with 'Research' is unlikely to result into any meaningful academic activity, thus in no way will benefit the students in any manner. Similarly, 2-year master's programme with the second year devoted entirely to research for those who have completed the 3-year bachelor's programme would do no good rather such a move will only deteriorate its quality. More appropriate would be to make bachelor's degree programme of 4-year duration, and both the years of master's programme devoted to the gaining of subject knowledge, with last semester both at the UG and PG levels also devoted for undertaking internship or research project of 9-10 credits. The new policy also has envisioned internships with local industry, businesses, artists, crafts persons, etc., as well as research internships with faculty and researchers at their own or other HEIs/research institutions, so that students may actively engage with the practical side of their learning and, as a by-product, further improve their employability. One also fails to understand the reasons for proposing 1-year master's programme for the students who have a 4-year bachelor's degree with 'Research'. Perhaps the policymakers have borrowed this idea from Western world without realising its impact on the quality of the master's programme. Besides, without having mastered the subject, admitting to Ph.D. programme with bachelor's degree would be unfeasible move because the students have not yet mastered the subject in which he or she will do research.

The youngsters out of higher secondary schools generally are not able to take a call on life's choices ahead. As such, apart from imparting in-depth knowledge of the discipline, HEIs have the responsibility in discovering their interests, nurturing their passions, and to counsel and guide these novice souls to navigate this new world full of opportunities. This is where 'Mentoring' and ‘Counselling’ comes into play. A close interaction with the mentors goes a long way in shifting gears from higher secondary school to the university and then to the world at large which is quite complex and challenging. In the Western world, Mentoring and Counselling has been formalised into the administrative system with a view that the students who are novices in all respects are mentored, guided and helped in nurturing their passions, emotional adjustments and managing stress. This equally important enabling mechanism is grossly missing in Indian HEIs, thus depriving students of this useful opportunity. It is pleasing to note that the new policy does make a mention of counselling to the students but without laying due emphasis. Besides, mentoring which is highly important ingredient of higher education ecosystem has been overlooked by the new policy. It is also a fact that without a policy direction, in view of great significance of counselling and mentoring, HEIs should at their own put in place systematized arrangement for mentoring and counselling of students.

7

Action Plan for the Implementation of Institutional and Faculty Autonomy Envisaged in National Higher Education Policy 2020

Offering greater autonomy to the Higher Education Institutions (HEIs) and its faculty is one of the important takeaways of the new policy. Autonomy is highly essential for HEIs to achieve excellence as it offers greater scope for creativity and innovation in all its spheres but with a caveat that there exists a ecosystem of people and systems capable of using it in an appropriate manner to yield due dividends. Besides, the wholehearted commitment and cooperation of the state governments to the new 'System of Governance' for HEIs would be critical. To seek the commitment and cooperation of the bureaucracy, it would need to be structured and implemented in a manner that takes care-off their concerns fully, however, without compromising with the spirit behind the autonomy envisioned in the new policy. Equally important would be its effective implementation and the appropriate checks and balances put in place to ensure greater transparency and accountability.

To govern effectively, educational institutions essentially would need Academic Autonomy, Administrative Autonomy, and Financial Autonomy. Academic autonomy refers to the freedom to decide about the new courses to be offered, course curriculum, teaching pedagogy, and assessment while as administrative autonomy is concerned with the freedom in manpower planning, appointments, promotions and other service matters. Financial autonomy is related to the freedom in planning and controlling its finance function of an organisation. All the three types of autonomy are interdependent, implying that in the absence of one, the others will fail to yield the desired results.

It is a fact that one of the reasons for under performance of the universities in the country has been the lack of autonomy to govern independently, free of any external interference. This problem is more prevalent in state universities. Universities in India are considered as autonomous institutions but the autonomy which was conceived by the architects of the university system in India, has got eroded over a period of time largely due to the failure of the Vice Chancellors to lead from the front with selfless devotion to pursue the institutional interests and partly due to the bureaucratisation of apex decision-making bodies of universities where bureaucrats are valued more than academicians. Therefore, envisaging greater autonomy through a system of graded accreditation, is one of the most important and meaningful recommendations of the new policy. Upon receiving the appropriate graded accreditation, a university can become self-governing institution through the Board of Governors (BoG) which will be empowered to govern the institution free of any external interference. If this recommendation is translated meaningfully and implemented in letter and spirit with the commitment of all, it will go a long way in helping the universities to achieve greater excellence. But the blueprint detailing out all the structural and operational aspects of a BoG are missing in the policy, therefore, necessitates to deliberate on the following pertinent questions:

- Who is empowered to constitute the BoGs initially?
- What shall be the size and composition of the board? Who will be its chairperson?
- Will there be nominated members of the state government/ HECI on the board?
- Whether the board would enjoy financial and administrative autonomy to the extent that its financial projections shall be binding on the government?

Since the selection of new members shall be carried out by the BoGs itself, therefore, the constitution of the initial board would determine the success or failure of succeeding boards because it is an established fact that incompetence or nepotism or favouritism would breed the same in the times to come. Therefore, apart from proven capabilities, people known for integrity and selfless devotion to the cause of equity and justice should be preferred. The size of the board should be proportionate to the size of the university in terms of number of faculties, campuses, affiliated/constituent colleges. It should mainly consist of academicians and technocrats representing the university, its affiliated and constituent colleges and at least 50% members should be from Civil Society and other institutions. There should be three nominated members of state governments of the rank of Commissioner Secretaries of the departments of Finance, Planning and Development and Higher Education on the board. The tenure of the non-permanent members should be three years.

The question is that should Chancellor and Pro-Chancellor form a part of the BoGs with Chancellor as its Chairperson? To ensure a balance of power, they may not be made a part of the BoGs, instead there should be 'Chancellors Committee' to oversee the functioning and performance of the university, which shall consist of Chancellor, Pro-Chancellor, Education Minister, Two nominated members of HECI, Chairperson of BoGs and Vice Chancellor of the university concerned and VCs of other sister universities. The Committee should meet annually under the chairpersonship of Chancellor to review the functioning of the university. The chairman shall be required to present before the Chancellors Committee 'Annual Performance Report', all audit reports along with action taken on the deviations reported by the auditors and Institutional Development Plans for approval. Besides, the powers to recommend amendments in the University Act shall vest with the Chancellors Committee only.

The BoGs should be the final authority to decide about all the matters of governance including creating new departments, launching new courses, approving revenue and capital expenditure budgets without any referrals to any outside agency or authority. Key to its success would lie in establishing effective ways to govern while respecting the autonomy of all stakeholders in decision-making with open communication with campus constituencies. It should act as both buffer and bridge between the university and outside agencies particularly Govt. Besides, to make its working smooth and meaningful, it should constitute four committees from the members of the BoGs, viz., Administrative Committee, Finance and Audit Committee, Academic Planning and Development Committee, and Building Committee. Matters pertaining to appointments, promotions, and other service matters should be routed through administrative committee while as budgets and internal & external audit reports should come through the Finance Committee. Similarly, proposals for establishing new departments/centres or starting new courses and annual academic audit reports should be placed before the Academic Planning and Development Committee through academic council. All construction proposals should have the approval of the Building Committee before placing in the meeting of BoGs for final approval.

The new policy aims at doing away with the system of affiliating colleges by upgrading the existing affiliated college into an 'Autonomous Degree Granting Colleges' (ADGCs) through a system of graded autonomy based on minimum accreditation benchmarks. After getting the status of ADGC, a college will enjoy academic autonomy to decide at its own through a well-established framework about all academic matters like courses to be offered, course curriculum, teaching pedagogy and assessment. This kind of autonomy to a great extent is being enjoyed by the affiliated colleges under the existing system but under the close supervision of the affiliating university. Therefore, it seems that it would serve little or no purpose. It is known to one and all that the affiliated colleges are marred mainly due to the infrastructural bottlenecks be it, physical infrastructure or human resources, and not by the lack of academic autonomy. The present state of affairs of the colleges is that the large number of colleges are mainly run by the contractual faculty. Granting academic autonomy only would result into more course offerings with an imminent causality of quality of education. To derive some benefit from the autonomous status, new policy should have also envisaged administrative and financial autonomy for such colleges.

With appropriate accreditations, new policy also allows ADGCs to evolve into research-intensive or teaching-intensive universities. This will result into mushrooming of the universities in the country. The existing policy of having few universities with affiliated or constituent colleges is more appropriate than having universities in every nook and corner. The mushrooming of universities would result into greater concentration of local students thus, defeating the very essence of the nomenclature of 'University' which implies a universe of diverse cultures, communities, races and religions. Diversity is highly important to ensure greater exposure and interaction among different cultures, religions, races, etc. which in turn results into greater cultural integration and assimilation thus, promotes global citizenship values.

Faculty in the university presently do enjoy academic autonomy, operated through a well-established framework of Board of Studies, Academic Council and Departmental Research Committees (DRCs) which are represented only by the faculty members. Faculty have the freedom to design their own curricular and pedagogical approaches, including textbook and reading material selections, the form of evaluation and assessment. But the autonomy comes with a greater responsibility for the faculty to use the granted authority for the greater good of the learners. Therefore, the question is that have we used this authority responsibly and in a meaningful manner. Unfortunately, most of the times, we have been found wanting while discharging the academic autonomy granted to us. In most of the cases, panel of experts nominated for these boards, or for evaluating theses generally includes friends rather than real experts. Have we ever made any attempt to adopt the best practices from the developed parts of the world? We continue to use the age-old teaching pedagogy and assessment. Our assessment system continues to remain heavily weighted towards summative semester-end written examination which we all know is a test of memory thus, fails to assess higher order abilities and other qualities. The new trend happening, is that the Boards of Studies and Academic Council which are cornerstones for ensuring effective learning, thus by all means are the most important academic bodies mandated to decide about all academic matters after thorough debate and discussion, are being made to follow directions coming from bureaucrats or some superficial committees.

Autonomy, a key to the achievement of greater excellence in higher education, has been explicitly emphasised in the new policy. But equally important is the element of accountability which is conspicuously missing in the new policy. It is known to one and all that the entire ecosystem in the country is beset with all sorts of malpractices or inefficiencies. It would be highly unrealistic to assume that the HEIs are immune to any such toxicity. Under the new policy, BoGs have been made responsible and accountable to the stakeholders through full online and offline public self-disclosure of all finances, audits, procedures, infrastructure, educational outcomes, etc. Though it is likely to serve little or no purpose yet, the disclosures need to be such which reflects performance across all parameters with minute details. Having well-established systems of annual audits in place namely Academic Audit, Management Audit, Financial Audit (Internal & External), Cost & Works Audit would enable to achieve the goals of efficiency and excellence, provided corrective actions are taken to plug the deviations. However, such audits except internal financial audit should be conducted by credible third parties on annual contract basis. Besides, best performers should be rewarded through fast-track promotions, or pay increases or by awarding medals/certificates which will induce greater competitiveness amongst the faculty/employees.

8

How to Integrate Vocational Education into Higher Education?

Education is an organised process, aimed to pass-on a body of knowledge/skill and develop character to make students qualified and competent to perform certain jobs in a desired manner. The education is classified into school education & higher education, professional & non-professional education and vocational education & academic education. All forms of education have relevance in the realm of socio-economic development, therefore, it would be wrong to overemphasise or under emphasise on any form of education. But in the past there was greater emphasis towards academic and technical education. However, with the sectoral transformation of economies where secondary and territory sectors have overtaken the primary sector, the need for skilled labour has increased which in turn has led to the significance of vocational and technical education. Traditionally vocational education was non-academic in nature and was totally related to a specific trade, occupation or vocation and was mainly concerned with preparing students for a specific trades, or crafts or as a technician. Over a period of time, it has become academic as well but involves less academic learning and is mainly focussed on manual or practical activities and training.

The history of vocational education in India dates back to 1964 when Kothari Commission concluded that many jobs do not require university education but such jobs can be performed by the higher secondary school students after being properly trained for such jobs. Although the focus on vocational education in India continued since long but during the last 7-8 years there has been greater push from the government towards this form of education. Many initiates at the government level were taken to widen the coverage of vocational education in the country. In 2014, GOI formed the Ministry of Skill Development & Entrepreneurship with the responsibility to coordinate skill development efforts across the country, building vocational & technical training framework, building new skills and innovative thinking etc. In 2015, the first Skill Development Mission was launched by GOI to provide an institutional framework to rapidly implement and scale-up skill development efforts across the country. It seeks to provide institutional capacity to train a minimum of 300 million people by the year 2022.

Even though there has been much stress on the vocational education during the last 7-8 years, India still lags behind most of the developed countries. Realising the slow progress in vocational education compared to the western world, NEP-2020 emphasises on the urgent need for reimagining the vocational education by exploring the reasons for not gaining much success in achieving the set targets. The primary reasons cited for this dismal performance includes:

- Vocational education has in the past focused largely on Grades 11-12 and on dropouts in Grade 8 and upwards.
- Students passing out from Grades 11-12 with vocational subjects often did not have well-defined pathways to continue with their chosen vocations in higher education.
- The admission criteria for general higher education were not designed to provide openings to students who had vocational education qualifications, leaving them at a disadvantage relative to their compatriots from 'mainstream' or 'academic' education.
- The vocational education is perceived to be inferior to mainstream education and meant largely for students who are unable to cope with the latter which to a great extent has affected the choices students make.

Given the above perceived bottlenecks, New Policy aims to overcome the social status hierarchy associated with vocational education and offers integration of vocational education programmes into mainstream education. Beginning with vocational exposure at early ages in middle and secondary school, quality vocational education will be integrated smoothly into higher education. The policy aims that every child learns at least one vocation and is exposed to several more. The new policy noted that by 2025, at least 50% of learners through the school and higher education system shall have exposure to vocational education, for which a clear action plan with targets and timelines will be developed. Vocational education will be integrated in the educational offerings of all secondary schools in a phased manner over the next decade. Towards this goal, secondary schools will also collaborate with ITIs, polytechnics, local industry, etc. Skill labs will also be set-up in the schools in a 'Hub and Spoke Model' which will allow other schools to use the facility.

NEP-2020 requires higher education institutions to offer vocational education either on their own or in partnership with industry and NGOs. As per the new policy, the B.Voc. degrees introduced in 2013 will continue to exist, but vocational courses will also be available to students enrolled in all other bachelor's degree programmes, including the 4-year multidisciplinary bachelor's programmes. Vocational courses were in the offing in the colleges under a sponsored scheme of UGC which remained in operation for few decades. Besides, under Choice Based Credit System, students at undergraduate level are offered skill courses with a huge basket of courses. It is also that the number of colleges have started offering certificate skill courses under various schemes of the GOI. But the question is "have such initiatives towards vocational education at higher education level really yielded the desired dividends? Although there has been no study so far to know the end results of these initiatives yet, there are clear indications that these initiatives have grossly failed either in skilling the students in real sense or helping them to get suitable jobs on the basis of such courses. What are the reasons for such failures need to be explored, otherwise the initiates offered in NEP-2020 are likely to meet the same fate.

The much talked about reasons for such failures are twofold; one the skill courses have been framed in a manner that many of them were not truly skill courses and also the course contents of many of such courses are found to be more of academic in nature than truly skill oriented. Second, these courses are being taught by the faculty who have no practical exposure thus, their pedagogy generally remains mainly academic rather than practical and experiential, thus defeats whatever little or more skill orientation such courses are carrying. To make vocationalisation of higher education really useful particularly in our union territory which is unique in many respects, in the first instance, there is a need to do "Skill Mapping" based on "Local Opportunities". The Skill Sector Councils (SSCs) have identified sector-wise skill courses with qualification paths and national occupation standards, but such skill courses are nation specific rather than area specific. Therefore, there is a need to constitute an expert committee to undertake a detailed "Skill Mapping" for each distinct geographical area to identify the skill courses to be focused at different levels of the education area-wise. The work already done by the SSCs can be taken as an important input by the committees for "Skill Mapping" of a given geographical area taking into account the local opportunities. In the Union Territory of J&K, job opportunities for skilled persons are generally limited for obvious reasons, therefore, while doing skill mapping, the committee should also consider the skills that are in high demand nationally and internationally, particularly in the gulf region. Equally important for the expert committee would be to identify the skills which can be aligned with the higher education either as embedded courses or standalone courses and the skills that can be exclusively acquired at ITIs, polytechnics and other technical institutions.

Equally important would be to design the course curriculum and teaching pedagogy in a manner that truly results into imparting the skill sets required in real life situations. Therefore, the committee in consultation with industry experts and academia should frame course contents for the skill courses to be adopted by higher educational institutions. The soft skill courses are more appropriate to be aligned with the higher education but to conduct such courses, mainly practitioners should be involved to educate and train the students. It would be more appropriate for HEIs to start certificate skill courses in association with the industry partners which should be aligned with the degree programmes in a manner that the students are able to get bachelor's degree along with the certificate skill course. Apprenticeship with the local industries should form an important part of the course curriculum of skill courses offered in a standalone basis or in an embedded form with the bachelor's degree programme. It would be also appropriate for HEIs to award certificate for skill courses along with the bachelor's degree which will enable them to claim an expertise in the skills acquired while seeking a job.

Kashmir has been famous throughout the world as much for its craftsmanship skills as for its physical charm and natural beauty. The craftsmanship skills continued passing on from generation to generation but this age-old industry of the state, which was enjoying prestige and unique place in the market, has lost lot of its sheen for varied reasons. But the most worrying aspect has been that the new generation is reluctant from taking-up these traditional vocations. There have been concerted efforts from the government to regain the past glory of this historical treasure. These efforts can be supplemented further through vocational education by encouraging the educated youth to get involved in this treasure trove by using modern means and methods of business. HEIs would need to design such courses on handicrafts in a manner that will educate the enterprising youth about the various crafts, their entrepreneurial potential and help them in taking these crafts to a different level of design development and marketing practices.

A well-established fact is that the success in initiating new policies and programmes depends on three things, viz., How realistically the new programmes/policies have been conceived and planned; How these have been implemented in letter & spirit and post-implementation whether a proper and thorough assessment has been made to know how far the desired results have been achieved. In our country, many policies and programmes fail to yield desired results due to faulty implementation wittingly or unwittingly. It is also that many a times we continue to pursue with wrongly conceived policies and programmes because we never bother to assess whether the policies have been successful in achieving the intended results. As a result, we continue to pump scarce financial resources without achieving due dividends. At times the assessment of policies and programmes is done just to complete the process without any honest intent. One of the fundamental principles of good governance is to continuously assess the progress of the policies and programmes in terms of intended outcomes so as to know that how far the intended goals have been achieved. Therefore, it will be of utmost importance for the policy makers to have a third-party assessment of the vocational education policies and programmes which would enable to align and realign our efforts to achieve intended outcomes.

9

Faculty as Catalysts for Advances in Quality Teaching and Research

A focus on quality teaching & learning; research & discovery; and outreach & engagement aiming to create, convey, and apply knowledge to expand personal growth and opportunity, advance social & community development, and foster economic competitiveness, generally is the vision/mission of universities in today's 'Knowledge Society' era. The main architects for achieving this noble vision are the faculty members who not only should be qualified to discharge their duties but also require to feel truly invested in, connected to, and committed to their institution and community. Equally important for them to be effective, is to demonstrate professional ethics in their pursuits continually. To have a committed and capable faculty with professional ethics, the need is to have an ecosystem which among other things should ensure the appointment of the "Best and the Brightest", greater autonomy to the faculty to do their jobs as effectively as possible and recognition of excellence in teaching and research. Besides, treating them as essential ingredients of our socio-economic set-up by ensuring respect, dignity, and due role in shaping the socio-economic destiny, would act as a great motivator. However, holding them accountable for not delivering on basic norms will be highly critical for achieving the set goals.

The recruitment process that is in place is not foolproof to ensure that every time only the "Best and the Brightest" gets appointed. Although the regulator has tried to bring greater objectivity into the appointment process yet, the lack of seriousness on the part of selection committees and nepotism/favoritism continues to impede the selection of the best. What matters the most is the resolve and commitment of Vice Chancellors to ensure the appointment of the brightest which unfortunately is missing, though not widely. Given such a scenario, there is an urgency to embrace the world's best practices regarding appointment and promotion of faculty. It would be in the fitness of things now to make Ph.D. with NET an essential qualification for the appointment of Assistant Professors with some minimum quality research output. Besides, the system of probation which was aimed to flush out the slippages if any at an early stage, has failed in its intended goal. Realising, this and other deficiencies, the new education policy has rightly suggested a system of multiple parameters for proper performance assessment, for the purposes of 'Tenure' i.e., confirmed employment after probation. Like in the western world, the confirmation of services after probation should be exclusively based on the 'Students Reviews and Peer Reviews'. The need is also to revisit the existing API system to make it more meaningful by exclusively focusing on teaching performance in terms of student reviews and peer reviews by independent experts, innovations in course curriculum, quality research output, professional development, collaborative research, extension and contribution to the corporate body.

Once the best faculty are appointed, they need an enabling ecosystem for their growth and development, the salient features of which include; the availability of requisite infrastructure, competitive culture and opportunities for growth and development. Systems of merit-based career management and progression would be a key to ensure greater commitment of faculty towards advancing his/her students, institutional, and their own professional growth. However, currently our universities are marred less by the availability of infrastructural facilities but more by the lack of greater autonomy and merit-based career management and progression. At the top of all this, the "Organisational Culture" mired by the toxicity of lobbyism, infighting and internal politics is very much prevalent in the universities. In such organisations, people generally invest in cultivating close relationships with top authorities one way or the other or seeking political support rather than trying to earn positions/promotions on the basis of his or her own merit at the huge cost of institutional efficiency. Such an "Organisational Culture" is found more prevalent in those universities whose leaders lacks 'Leadership in Integrity' and 'Leadership in Excellence'. Such academic leaders find refuge in creating and revolving around Coteries and psychophants who have rotten the basic foundations of such important institutions.

To take care-off the factors that lie behind low faculty motivation and commitment, NEP-2020 offers number of recommendations. The new policy without mentioning optimum workload, emphasizes that the teaching duties should not be excessive, and student-teacher ratios also not too high, so that the activity of teaching remains pleasant and there is adequate time for interaction with students, and for conducting research. The current weekly direct teaching-learning hours for Assistant Professors and Associate Professors/Professors are 16 hours and 14 hours respectively, should be reduced to 12 hours for all the categories, which should include 4 hours per week for research supervision/mentoring for Associate Professors/Professors and 2 hours per week for guiding and counselling for Assistant Professors. Besides, in no case, an Assistant Professor should be asked to teach more than two different subjects. The new policy also lays emphasis on the greater autonomy to the faculty in designing curricular, pedagogical approaches and assessment to offer them more freedom to innovate and be creative. The most important takeaway of the new policy is the emphasis on the recognition of excellence through fast-track promotion for recognizing high impact research, appropriate rewards, recognitions, and movement into institutional leadership. This will surely result into greater competitive culture within the institution, thus better output, provided it is formalised and implemented in an appropriate manner. For this purpose, a system of multiple parameters for proper performance assessment has been suggested, including peer and student reviews, innovations in teaching pedagogy, quality and impact of research, professional development activities, and service to the institution.

Faculty in the universities presently do enjoy academic autonomy, operated through a well-established framework of Board of Studies, Academic Council and DRCs which are represented only by the faculty members. Faculty have the freedom to design their own curricular, pedagogical approaches, and assessment. But this autonomy foists greater responsibility on the faculty to use the authority granted for the greater good of the learners. Therefore, the question is 'Have we used this authority responsibly and in a meaningful manner?' Unfortunately, most of the times, the faculty have been found wanting while using the 'Academic Autonomy' granted to them. In most of the cases, panel of experts nominated for these boards, or for evaluating theses generally includes friends rather than true experts. Have we ever made any attempt to adopt the best practices from the developed parts of the world. We continue to use the age-old teaching pedagogy and assessment. Our assessment system continues to remain heavily weighted towards summative semester-end written examination which we all know is a test of memory thus, fails to assess higher order abilities and other qualities. The Boards of Studies and Academic Council which are cornerstones for effective teaching-learning environment, thus by all means the most critical academic bodies mandated to decide about academic matters after thorough debate and discussion, however, unfortunately such critical decision-making bodies are being muffled to follow directions, coming from bureaucrats or some superficial committees. Strong urge to innovate and change for the greater good of the learners and the institution, unfortunately is found largely missing which has been the root cause for the failures to make greater strides in quality teaching and research by most of the HEIs. This sad state of affairs calls for greater accountability of the faculty and these crucial academic bodies.

In the introduction to NEP-2020, it is passionately argued that the new policy must help to re-establish teachers, at all levels, as the most respected and essential members of our society. But unfortunately, in the new policy there is no mention of how to re-establish teachers. Gone are the days when teachers were revered the most as were being considered an embodiment of thorough knowledge, intellect, integrity and selfless devotion to the greater good of the society regardless of caste, colour, creed, and status. A Million Dollar question for all of us is that why the contemporary teachers are not being looked through the same lens by the society today even though being more qualified than the teachers of olden days. The most prominent reason for all this has been that the teachers of the olden days were found immune to all sorts of toxicity existing in the society but unfortunately the contemporary teachers have lost that immunity, thus got infected from all sorts of viruses plaguing the society at large. Today's teachers in general are lacking professional ethics and commitment to the greater good of their students and the society at large. Unfortunately, these knowledge creators and disseminators have also been swept away by the wave of materialism thus have turned from "Selfless to Selfish Souls". It is sad to note that to pursue their individual goals, the contemporary teachers are found to go to any extent regardless of consequences for their learners and the institution. The university teachers consider themselves as 'Intellectuals', rightly so, as being highly qualified people in the entire society, but the tag of intellectualism foists a greater responsibility to stand for truth, equity, and justice which unfortunately is lacking in most of them, thus have rendered their intellectualism of little or no meaning for their students, institutions and the society.

The blame for all this alone cannot lie on the teachers but more on the society as whole. When the society at large has lost value for honesty, piety, justice and equity, therefore, it is unrealistic to expect the teachers to be immune to such social evils when they are the part and parcel of the larger society. But still, had there been no medaling in the affairs of these "Unique Universes", the situation would not have been as bad as it is today. Like the western world, if the establishment would have allowed these autonomous institutions to function without interference, the situation would have been largely under control. Besides, the establishment which is mainly dominated by the bureaucrats, who unfortunately have failed to acknowledge that these intellectuals are capable to complement their efforts in finding plausible solutions to the various issues confronting the economies and the societies. This calls for the change of mindset of the establishment about these intellectuals by accepting the reality that they truly deserve a "Place of Pride" in public policy making like in the western world. Unlike the developed parts of the world, the role of technocrats is grossly missing in the governance, and is solely in the hands of 'Parochial Bureaucrats' who are 'Jack of All Trades' but 'Masters of None'. Those who have the knowledge and expertise, have been rendered powerless for being labeled as mere academicians, but the fact is that they are specialists in their chosen areas of specializations, possessing "Intellectual Capital" which would be of immense use for the greater good of our economies and societies. However, conferring the "Place of Pride" to these intellectuals in public policy making will have to be with a 'Caveat' that the 'Home of these Intellectuals' i.e. universities would need total transformation by reinventing their operational methodologies based on the world's best practices in teaching and research. The onus for all this will lie on the Regulator/Government, however, the role of 'Institutional Leaders' would be highly critical. Unless and until the leadership crisis with which these institutions are largely marred, not taken care of, instead of reclaiming a 'Place of Pride', these would decay beyond any repair.

10

Internationalisation of Indian Education: Will it Arrest Brain Drain & Make India a Hub for International Students?

India continues to suffer socio-economically from the 'Brain Drain' even though it witnessed transformation of its economy from the status of underdeveloped to the most important emerging economy in the world. Indian is aiming to become a five trillion-dollar economy by 2024 but unfortunately in the absence of better opportunities, millennials in good numbers are leaving the country to fulfil their lifelong dreams in the western world. It is estimated that close to 200,000 students go abroad every year for higher education having an estimated outflow of ₹ 50,000 crores per annum. The outflow of such a huge amount of money would have been no concern at all, if after completing education they have been returning back to serve their homeland, but hardly anybody returns. Among other things, the problem of 'Brain Drain' has been largely due to the lack of world class educational pursuits and better professional prospects in the country. It is not only the students who go abroad for higher education, there are large number of professionals also who goes abroad for further education and lifelong settlement in the western world. This 'Brain Drain' helps the host countries in all respects at the huge socio-economic costs to the countries where from 'Brain Drain' takes place.

Since long the 'Brain Drain' has been viewed as a problem by the politicians and policy makers, to be tackled for the larger good of the country but without any success at all. The phenomenal economic growth which the country witnessed during the last 10 to 12 years, has also failed even to slow the rate of 'Brain Drain'. There has been persistent growth in the 'Brain Drain' from India across international borders to Canada, America, Australia, European and other countries. The NEP-2020 among other things has emphasised on the 'Internationalisation of Indian Education' with twin goals to achieve; one, to make India a hub for international students as well as provide greater mobility to Indian students who may wish to study at, transfer credits to, or carry out research abroad, and vice versa. Towards the attainment of these aspirational goals, the NEP-2020:

- Lays emphasis for the universities to offer courses in subjects, like Indology, AYUSH systems of medicine, yoga, arts, etc. to attract international students towards these and other courses.
- Aims India to sign mutually beneficial MOUs with foreign countries to facilitate research/teaching collaborations and faculty/student exchanges.
- Allows high ranking Indian universities to set-up campuses in other countries, and similarly, the top 100 global universities will be facilitated to operate in India.
- Offers opportunity of transfer of credits acquired in foreign universities as per the requirements of each HEI, and counted for the award of a degree.

To allow and facilitate top 100 global universities to establish campuses in India and also the permission to transfer credits acquired in foreign universities, is believed by many to offer opportunities for world class educational pursuits well within India, thus help to tackle the age-old problem of 'Brain Drain'. Politicians and many academicians have exhibited exuberance and confidence that the steps taken in the NEP-2020 will not only make India as a hub for international students but will stop Indian students going abroad as the world class educational opportunities will be available right here. Honourable Prime Minister while addressing the Governors/State Governments conference, has said that NEP-2020 will help to tackle the problem of 'Brain Drain' from India, once top 100 global universities will set-up campuses in India, as the students would not need to travel abroad anymore. He further lamented that with the entry of top global universities in the country, the competitive culture among HEIs will improve for the greater good of the students. Similar views were expressed by Union Education Minister while addressing 8th convocation ceremony of IIT Indore. While elaborating, he had said that we are going to strengthen parameters under our "Stay in India" campaign for which research will be put on the fast track under NEP-2020. It is not only the government functionaries showing such exuberance, but the heads of many academic institutions are highly optimistic about the new policy, helping in arresting the 'Brain Drain'.

The exuberance shown by the government functionaries and others about the potential of NEP-2020 to make India as a hub of the international students and in putting a break on 'Brain Drain' by stopping Indian students to go abroad, realistically speaking it is more in "Rhetoric Than In Reality". A strong push by the government and the HEIs will help in getting international students but not in large numbers and that too generally from Africa and some South Asian countries. Why students from all over the world prefer to go to the western world? It is not only in the search of world class education but more for an opportunity to settle in the western world, promising better professional prospects and better quality of life. Such an opportunity will not be available to the foreign students in India, thus will act as an impediment to compete with the western world. The students from the above-mentioned countries will come to India for the reasons, one; that the quality of education available in India, is better than in their own countries and more for being less expensive than the universities in the western world. However, a rigorous admission criterion and more exclusive policies of the state governments, will act as a strong barrier to the entry of foreign students particularly in professional courses.

Allowing top global universities to set-up campuses, in reality will offer an opportunity only to the students belonging to the higher strata of the society for one simple reason that such institutions will charge exorbitant fee which will be beyond the capacity of the students belonging to middle and other lower classes. Besides, it is not yet clear whether the top global universities which will establish campuses here, will have to abide by the reservation policy in vogue in the country. Unless and until, the government makes it mandatory for such universities to abide by the reservation policy in admissions and offer some concession in admission fee to the students belonging to lower strata of society, such a move will not be inclusive rather exclusive, which would be violative of the NEP-2020 which lays greater emphasis on inclusiveness and equity in higher education. To meet this cherished goal of the new policy, such institutions should be made to abide by the reservation policy in admissions. Besides, Government of India would need to put in place a financial mechanism to either meet fully or partly the fee of the students belonging to the socially and economically disadvantaged groups of the society.

The Million Dollar Question is "Will the establishment of campuses by the top 100 global universities in India put breaks on the 'Brain Drain'? The answer is most likely No. The fact is that the Indian students are going abroad not only in search for world class education but more importantly for the reason to have a lifelong settlement in the host countries. The dream to settle in those countries is driven by the existence of very rewarding and conducive ecosystem consisting of better career opportunities, better standard of living, better quality of life, higher salaries, access to advanced technology, and universal human values of truth, righteous conduct, scientific temper, citizenship values. Unfortunately, all these opportunities and necessities of life are largely missing in our country. Otherwise no person with even an average IQ would never like to leave their mother land. It is not only that such opportunities are lacking here but one is generally made to face frustrating and inhuman onslaughts in day-to-day life here. No intelligent and sensitive person can bear to live under such stressful conditions thus, happily prefers to leave to have a better and secure future for himself and for his or her future generations abroad. Many professionals in the past tried to return home to serve their own people, but after having made to suffer all sorts of onslaughts, most of them finally returned back with a regret and great disappointment. So expecting that with the establishment of campuses by the top global universities will put breaks on the students moving abroad, would be surely an unrealistic expectation. It is expected that even those who will seek admissions in these universities, most of them would ultimately move out of the country in search of lucrative careers.

Brain drain is surely an important socio-economic problem, but India has largely been the causality of much more serious problem, which needs an attention of all of us, which is the "*Internal Brain Drain*". It is a fact that all the good brains do not move out, large numbers stays here, who unfortunately are made to suffocate and are generally pushed "*Down the Drain*". Unfortunately, almost all institutions whether, political, social, cultural, educational, economic, etc. which provide direction for development, have degenerated into monumental incompetence and malpractices. India is still in the category of most corrupt countries of the world. The Annual Corruption Perception Index (CPI), put out by Transparency International in 2019, out of 180 countries, India has been ranked at the 80th position. There is no denying the fact that the country suffers from all sorts of inefficiencies, misplaced priorities and malpractices like widespread nepotism, favouritism and corruption, the causality of all this cancerous situation in the country have been the meritorious and honest people. People working in different organisations are not paid for performance but for longevity and conventionality. More unfortunate is that the people are generally elevated to higher or leadership positions not because of their merit, achievements and integrity & honesty but for their affiliations and connections with those who are sitting in the power corridors. The height of the things in the country is that the institutions like universities which were considered temples of intellectualism, honesty, fair play, justice and equity have been polluted to an extent that the merit, performance and personal integrity have been made to go down the drain by most of the Institutional Heads who are generally appointed purely due to their political connections rather than being distinguished persons with impeccable track record of integrity and performance.

Meritorious and honest people are generally pushed to the margin and there seems to be the sanction from the power corridors to violate rules and regulations with impunity. In such a scenario, if Hargobind Khorana, Subramanya Chandersekhar, Amartya Sen and Abhijit Banerjee would not have decided to move out of the country, they would not have won the Nobel Prizes while staying in India. If the country has to prosper and grow, the only thing that needs to be done is to "Wage A War" without any discrimination against the malpractices of nepotism, favouritism and corruption which are rampant particularly in our state.

11
Catalysing Quality Research in Indian Universities

Research aiming to explore new frontiers in sciences and socio-economic domains is highly critical for growth and development in different spheres of life. Higher education institutions are considered ideal places for conducting research, which on the one hand would help country to invent new technologies/ solutions to socio-economic problems being faced and on the other hand helps in providing quality education. Evidence from the world's best universities throughout the history has shown that the best teaching and learning processes at the higher education level occur in environments where there is also a strong culture of research and knowledge creation. But merely conducting research serves little or no purposes, what matters the most, is the quality of research? Conducting cutting edge research in the areas of biotechnology, nanotechnology, artificial intelligence, etc. is important for the country like India, which is striving hard to get a place of prominence at the global stage.

India is confronted with number of challenges like, pollution, poverty & inequality, regional imbalances, environmental degradation, etc. All these and other problems necessitate universities to conduct quality and actionable research to mitigate various problems being confronted by the economy/society. A robust ecosystem for research is perhaps more important than ever with the rapid changes occurring in the world today, e.g., in the realm of climate change, population dynamics and management, biotechnology, and the rise of machine learning and artificial intelligence. Since the last few decades, universities in India have been placing greater emphasis in the conduct of research, however, still our universities have to go a long way, particularly in terms of quality of research.

Most talked about issue, particularly among academicians is the lack of funding for conducting quality research. The lack of funding is also being attributed in NEP-2020 as one of the reasons for the lack of sufficient and quality research in the Indian Universities. There are no two opinions about the lack of requisite funding for conducting research which is amply clear while comparing funding towards research in India with the developed countries of the world. As compared to 2.8% in USA, 4.3% in Israel and 4.2% in South Korea, only 0.69% of GDP is being invested in research in India. But given the huge commitments towards the social sector, it would be highly unrealistic to expect India to match developed countries when it comes to the funding of research. So whatever little or more funding is available, the funding agencies and the researchers are duty bound to use those funds most effectively in order to derive maximum dividends. To grow and catalyze quality research, in addition to the host of institutions that currently fund research, NEP-2020 has recommended the establishment of National Research Foundation (NRF), aimed to provide a reliable base of merit-based peer-reviewed research funding, and by undertaking major initiatives to seed and grow research at state universities where research capability is currently limited.

Establishment of NRF most likely would end up to the extent of an addition of one more institution, funding peer-reviewed grant proposals. It is good to try to address the problem of the lack of sufficient funding but it was equally important to address the other issues inhibiting the conduct of quality research of international standards in the Indian universities. The formulators of NEP-2020 were also required to seek an answer to a 'Million Dollar Question' that is, "Has the funding that has gone into the research so far, yielded the due dividends to the nation, if not, why?" On an average, every year ₹ 4500 to ₹ 5000 crores goes into the funding of research, such an amount is not little by all standards. With this amount, every year, the nation would have established one large university or a large hospital. There is no denying the fact that the quality of research conducted in Indian universities is far from satisfactory by all standards which is evident from the very dismal performance of the Indian universities in the global rankings. None of the Indian universities figure in the list of top 200 global universities mainly for the lack of quality research. UGC recently invited proposals to retrospectively assess the quality of Ph.D. theses awarded by the country's universities over the past 10 years. The fundamental reason for undertaking such a massive exercise cited by the UGC is to address the rampant allegations and concerns being raised globally over the quality of published papers and Ph.D. theses of Indian researchers.

There are no two opinions that the quality of research in Indian universities is marred by many other factors. Unless and until those factors are identified and addressed holistically, even increased allocations towards the conduct of research will do little or no good. The ecosystem for research in Indian universities is also constrained by the expected role failure of funding agencies, universities, subject experts and the researchers. Funding agencies have failed to liaison between researchers and relevant branches of government as well as industry, so as to allow breakthroughs to be optimally brought into public policy making. Besides, funding is done without making any honest and meaningful outcome-based assessment of the research, as a result of which many inefficiencies have blurred the landscape of research. It is in view of these facts that the public investment of Billions and Billions of rupees that has gone into the research so far, has failed to yield concrete results whatsoever. This is explicitly evident from the fact that the huge research conducted in Indian universities has hardly led into any significant technological breakthroughs, when universities are the only places where the solutions to the various challenges and issues being faced by the country are to be found. Since at the huge expense of socially and economically backward sections of the society, tax payers money is invested in the conduct of research, therefore, it was all the more important for the funding agencies and the universities to see that the funds provided are optimally used to achieve a greater good of the country. But unfortunately reckless funding is being done by the funding agencies without making any objective assessment of the funded research in terms of the intended outcomes in a transparent manner. As a result, there are widespread speculations of financial improbity in funded research which if true, unfortunately implies that the rot has infected the foundations of the temples of "Intellectual Curiosity, Honesty, Pity, Equity and Justice". In the absence greater transparency and accountability, such speculations are bound to take place.

Achieving greater heights in research to a great extent depends upon the professional ethics and inquisitive behaviour of the researchers. It is this lack of intellectual curiosity, no other scientist from India has received Nobel Prize after C.V. Raman. Unlike true scientists or researchers like C.V. Raman, unfortunately, the research in Indian universities to a majority of the researchers have become a "Mere Means to an End Rather Than an End in Itself". Generally so-called scientists/researchers in Indian universities have been found toiling hard to gain administrative positions which is unheard in the universities of Western World where all breakthroughs in technologies, sciences or social sciences has taken place. This is reflective of the lack of passion for research in our researchers. It is also true that the researchers cannot solely be blamed for such a sad scenario. Actually the rot lies in the overall ecosystem in which the academicians/researchers are made to work. Unlike the Western World, the academicians/researchers are deprived of their due role in shaping the socio-economic destiny of the country. There is a complete divorce between the systems of public policy making/governance and the research being done in the universities. There is a need to re-establish academicians/researchers in the country, at all levels, as the most respected and essential members of our society and of public policy making, because they truly shape our next generation of citizens and are capable of acting as a catalysts for effective policy making and governance.

It pains to say that gone are the days when academicians were known not only for the knowledge, they posses but equally for their commitment to professional ethics, and selfless devotion to their duties. Such professors have become very rare in our country. It is because of these unscrupulous elements, the quality of research has deteriorated to a great extent in Indian universities. It is also a fact that there are many scrupulously honest and meritorious academicians but unfortunately due to the widespread nepotism, favouritism and corruption which has pervaded all our institutions, are pushed to the margin. So unless and until the intuitions' whether educational or regulatory places premium only on merit, performance and integrity, things are not going to change. Rather, if we continue to operate with the current corrupt and inefficient systems, things are going to get bad to worse regardless of how much more we are going to invest in the education.

The most important "Silver Lining in the Cloud" is that there is no dearth of scholars and academicians having great intellect and passion for enquiry. The only problem is that we have failed to provide them a very stimulating and rewarding ecosystem. The key elements of an enabling ecosystem for research and development includes; well defined research policy both at the university and funding agency levels, administrative flexibility and support for quality research, mentoring of young researchers, greater focus on collaborative research, incentivisation of the conduct of high quality research and the availability of seed capital for incubation and innovations. The institutions should prioritise its research by focussing first on the local issues and challenges, followed by national level and global issues. The key to success would greatly lie in "Research Audit" conducted regularly, however, quality of research needs to be redefined in the context of changing global realities.

Universities in India have lost some sheen in the public view for obvious reasons. To regain lost public faith and image, there is an urgent need to improve the quality of research conducted in the universities, which among other things requires to redefine the measures of research quality. Currently "Bibliometrics" like; 'h-index' or quantitative methods such as, 'Citations or Journal Impact Factor' are taken as reliable measures of research quality. Critics have argued that time has come to move beyond these quantitative methods towards more qualitative or outcome-based measures. Besides, "Bibliometrics" tools are found to be indicators of quality in some areas of social sciences, such as psychology and economics but not in many applied or policy related areas. In the changing landscape of higher education, it is vociferously argued that we need to embrace "Altmetrics" which are qualitative and outcome based. These include 'Citations in Public Policy Documents; Part of Industry Practices, Patents; Discussions on Research Blogs; Main Stream Media Coverage; Bookmarks or Reference Managers. Since these measures are outcome based, therefore, are sure to bring researchers nearer to the real world, which in turn will bring universities and its researchers into the greater public viewing.

12

Whether Online Teaching-Learning Process and Evaluation is a Perfect Alternative to the Off-Line Mode?

An immediate response to deal with the Covid-19 pandemic was the imposition of lockdown. Now in almost all parts of the world, restrictions on the movement of people and in the conduct of business activities by and large have been lifted. Although all sectors of socio-economic life have partially or fully resumed with well laid down SOPs but all the educational institutions still remains closed. New normal in the educational sector has been to conduct classes and examinations online. The jury about this 'New Normal' happening right from school education to higher education is divided. One group of people have readily accepted this new normal while as, the other group is questioning its efficacy. This difference of opinion calls for a critical review of the opposing viewpoints to reach to a logical conclusion about the issue.

During the lockdown all the socio-economic activities remained suspended but the activity of teaching particularly at higher education level continued through online. Social media was a buzz showing someone conducting online classes from the isolation ward of a COVID hospital and someone sitting at the top of a tree to get connected for online classes. Due to over exuberance and enthusiasm, many institutions have started offering even online courses. Notable thing has been the conduct of webinars' which is taking the teaching fraternity by storm and everybody is plunging into it.

Multi Dollar question is "Whether Online Teaching is Offering a Perfect Alternative to the Off-Line Teaching"? The protagonists of online teaching-learning process contend that it serves the purpose of education as effectively as off-line teaching and in fact sometimes better than the regular mode of teaching. It is also being argued that online mode of education enables a student to move at his or her own convenient pace to learn the subject as it allows to revisit recorded lectures again and again which is not possible in the off-line mode of learning. Besides, online lectures supplemented by Chat Groups, Video Meetings, Google Chats and Document Sharing has been argued to have enabled teachers to reach out to the students more effectively. However, some protagonists of online teaching do agree that in addition to the problem of huge digital divide, the online teaching cannot truly replicate off-line teaching as it lacks in one important aspect, i.e. the benefits of peer learning. But to them there is no other alternative to save the precious time of the students other than the mode of online education.

A glaring issue for online education during this pandemic has been the assessment of students. Online examination poses issues of ethical behaviour and integrity. It is most likely that appearing in the online examination while sitting at home, students will resort to unfair means. To overcome the issue of unethical behaviour, proponents of online education find solution in open book examination. Besides, software enabled proctored online examination is being talked about as a possible solution to check the unethical behaviour of students while assessing them from their homes. There are companies which offer camera-based face and body tracking devices with frequent camera scans of surroundings. Some companies even tout the use of artificial intelligence to detect if one is doing anything wrong.

The teaching fraternity by and large are not ready to accept online teaching to be a perfect alternative to 'Chalk-and-Talk System' of teaching-learning process. Antagonists of online education have cited various flaws which according to them render online teaching-learning process infructuous like; for both to the teacher and the tutor delivering or listening a live lecture becomes boring and monotonous. There is lack of eye contact which is essential to scan the mental state of students, as such a teacher is unable to decide whether to repeat or reorient the material which is easily possible in face-to-face teaching-learning system. Besides, it has been observed that most of the students just keep their devices on record mode without being physically present thus, makes it much harder to provoke or sustain discussion which is at the core of teaching-learning process. It is also being contended that chat boards and discussion fora's simply cannot replace with same efficacy the physical tutorials and even badinage or cajoling.

Most serious limitation with online teaching is with respect to the courses where laboratory work is essential ingredient. Yes simulated practical's or dummy data can be used to train students but the significance of hands-on-training cannot be replicated by any means. The antagonists of online teaching believe that it is not possible for conducting live practical's hence, students are not able to physically visualize and prove a point. The medical and other technical students are the worst hit as their hands-on-training cannot be replicated by any means. Medicos and Engineering students cannot do the clinical classes and active learning, so important for honing out their skills. The element of dirty hands in such streams has such a huge significance which under no circumstances can be underestimated.

Digital divide is being referred as one of the most serious constraint to online education. There is large chunk of population who are unable or struggle to participate in digital learning without any access to internet or technology. Greater emphasis towards online education by the government without any advance preparations have made the people belonging to the weaker sections of the society extremely worried for their wards, feeling to have been excluded as their children are unable to participate in online education for want of requisite technology/internet. According to *Tribune News Services*, a poor man namely Kuldip Kumar of Gummer village in Jwalamukhi had to sell his cow for ₹ 6,000 for buying a Smartphone for online studies of his two sons. It cannot be treated as an isolated case but digital divide in India is really huge.

Jury is out to pronounce whether online teaching can be a perfect alternative to the off-line teaching? Higher education is fundamentally aimed to: Educate and train students to make them professionally qualified to manage different spheres of life efficiently and effectively; Develop higher values of life like; moral and intellectual values, faith in brotherhoodism regardless of race, colour, religion, sex; Develop right attitudes and interest for leadership in public life. There is no possibility of developing higher values of life and potential leaders to lead professions and public life through online system of education because the achievement of these equally important goals requires intense interaction, debate & discussion, socio-cultural assimilation and greater exposure to the challenging real-world settings. Even the goal of gaining holistic view of the subject knowledge cannot be fully realised through online teaching happening in the present form as being deficient in many respects. Those who argue that there is no option other than to conduct online classes to save the precious time of students cannot be agreed upon as there is no scope for 'Something is Better Than Nothing' in education. One will be able to discharge his professional duties only when he or she is fully equipped with the knowledge and skill set required for the job. In the larger interest of education, more appropriate would have been to declare one semester a 'Zero Session' at least at higher education level.

Online system of education could have surely proved of some help if done with advance planning and through e-classrooms fitted with cameras and real Black-White Board. But sudden move without any advance planning, training and preparations towards online classes by all means is bound to cause very poor user experience and acceptance. There is no denying the fact that offline and e-learning can complement each other. It has been suggested to use "Flipped Classroom Technique" where students are provided notes and pre-recorded lectures in advance and have discussion/debate to clear doubts in the offline or online class. A blended mode of online and offline teaching learning and evaluation mode seems to be the best solution to get the maximum from both the systems.

SECTION THREE

Leadership and Governance

- Leadership Crisis in Indian Universities: Where the Rot Lies?
- Appointment of Vice Chancellors in Indian Universities: Calls for a Procedural Rejig
- Leadership Qualities of Successful Vice Chancellors in the Indian Context
- Planning and Assessing Institutional Effectiveness: Panacea for all Ills in Higher Education in India
- Evaluation of Teaching by Students: A Controversial Issue in Higher Education in India
- Integrating Formative, Continuous and Comprehensive Assessment System into Higher Education

13

Leadership Crisis in Indian Universities: Where the Rot Lies?

Institutions whether, political, economic, educational provide direction for development in all spheres of life. But the success or failure of these and other institutions greatly depends on the leadership with which endowed, as leaders being the centres around whom all others congregate. Although the existence of outstanding leaders is extremely important for the success of all institutions yet, the criticality of leadership in universities is more pervasive as it acts like a pivot around which rotates the entire edifice. As being cornerstone of an institution on which learning communities function and grow, these can make or mar an university. What makes one an outstanding academic leader is the pertinent question? An outstanding academic leader is the one who:

- Is visionary and demonstrates energy and commitment to the vision/mission of the university continually.
- Displays high moral standards in all spheres of governance. Great leaders are found to have a selfless devotion to the institutional goals. Only such leaders are widely trusted and respected, thus able to inspire others to work for the greater good of the institution.
- Places a premium only on merit, performance and personal integrity and strives for excellence in everything they do.

What is the current state of leadership and governance in our universities? The NEP-2020 has categorically stated that the universities in the country have also been the causality of suboptimal governance and leadership. As a consequence of poor leadership, our universities have failed to apply all the times highest professional and ethical standards, thus were unable to achieve excellence at par with the international standards. As per the QS World University Ranking-2021, none of the Indian Universities/Institutes could feature in the top 100, a total of 8 Institutes have found their place in the top 500, all these are IITs and IISc Bangalore. Such a gloomy picture is a reflection of poor performance of our universities at the global stage. The much talked about reason for such a gloomy picture has been the absence of outstanding and enthusiastic institutional leaders that cultivate excellence and innovation in their respectively universities. Thus the question arises, "Do We Have a Dearth of Outstanding Academic Leaders?" The fact is that India has a flair of talent comparable with the best in the world but during the last few decades, ordinary people have been found occupying the chair of Vice Chancellors. Surely with exceptions political interference in the selection of Vice Chancellors is being attributed to such a sad scenario. The rot mainly lies in the search committees which largely have failed to search and select the outstanding persons as Vice Chancellors, who not only are distinguished academicians but have a clear vision/mission and at the top of everything have a proven track record of administrative abilities and personal integrity and honesty.

It is sad to state that the 'Academic Leaders' who were known for their ethical conduct, professional ethics, and strong commitment to the greater good of the institutions, many of them are now found to have degenerated into monumental incompetence and corruption. Now it is common to see that the Vice Chancellors and top officers of the universities remains in the news less for the good they do, but more for the alleged corruption charges and other misdeeds. Very recent cases have been, the removal of Delhi University's Vice Chancellor for alleged violation of administrative rules and regulations. As per the news report of Nov. 25, 2020 (*Hindustan Times*), UGC has formed a 4-member panel to probe into the allegations of financial and administrative irregularities against the Vice Chancellor, Jamia

Hamdard University. Bihar's new Education Minister, Mr. Mewalal Choudhary had to resign hours after assuming charge for his alleged involvement in the corruption case when he was Vice Chancellor, Bihar Agriculture University. In 2019, in the conference of Vice Chancellors, Mr. Purohit, Hon. Governor, Tamil Nadu said that it was a blot on our civilisation to see Vice Chancellors and university professors being prosecuted for corruption. He further stated that vigilance raids on 2 former Vice Chancellors, the arrest of a sitting Vice Chancellor and the suicide committed by a former registrar in the last two years bears testimony to the worsening conditions of universities (Rohan Premkumar, 20th Dec. 2019, *The Hindu*). These are not isolated cases but the problems of corruption and other malpractices by top authorities in the universities are achieving serious dimensions day-by-day. The fact is that only a tip of the iceberg comes into the public notice. The misuse of powers and the irregularities committed by many Vice Chancellors does not come into public notice either due to their strong connections with the powerful politicians/investigating agencies or people privy to their misdeeds fear to report their wrongdoings for one or the other reasons. More shocking behaviour on their part has been that many Vice Chancellors, contrary to their sworn duty to see that the provisions of the Act, the Statutes and the Regulations are faithfully observed, have been found themselves violating the rules and regulations at will.

The rot actually lies in the community of academicians, majority of whom are found to have lost ethical behaviour, and more importantly professional ethics. Nowadays you will find professors going to any extent to seek favours for getting appointed as Vice Chancellors or to some other top administrative position. Ironically even those who consider themselves as great scientists or researchers, are being found in the forefront in this rat race. Actually, these so-called great scientists or researchers, are not the scientists out of passion for research but involve in the conduct of research as a "Mere Means to an End Rather Than an End in Itself". Lobbying by the professors to seek help from politicians and other power corridors has become the new normal for getting appointed as Vice Chancellors. As a result, the general belief in the academia is that unless and until one is politically connected or enjoys a favour of the lobbies, there is little or no scope to get appointed as Vice Chancellor regardless of one's impeccable track record of performance and personal integrity. More shocking is that there are widespread speculations that the monetary considerations are nowadays involved in the appointment of Vice Chancellors. A study conducted by five former Vice Chancellors and 20 Professors has revealed that over 65% of stakeholders believe that Vice Chancellor posts are filled on "Quid-Pro-Quo Basis" (75% of VCs Unfit to Hold Post: Study; *Times News Network*). If this is true, unfortunately, it reveals that the rot has infected the basic foundations of our universities which were considered 'Temples' of "Intellectual Curiosity, Honesty, Pity, Equity and Justice".

It takes "Two to Tango" i.e. the senior academicians alone cannot be held responsible for the above sad state of affairs prevailing in the country. Equally responsible, for all this undesirable behaviour on the part of some senior academicians has been the selection procedures that are in vogue for the appointment of Vice Chancellors. Had the search-cum-selection committee members been conscientious of their sworn duties, no authority whatsoever would have been able to influence their selections. It is not only the problem of political interference but the more chilling fact is that the search committees have been found to have failed to discharge this crucial responsibility honestly and professionally. Number of times it has been seen that no scientific criteria is being followed while short listing the candidates, rather a pick and choose policy followed. In some cases, it has been found that short listing and final selection has been done merely on the basis of research output/research funding generated as if they are appointing somebody to conduct research when the fact is that the Vice Chancellor is only mandated to govern the administrative affairs by offering Leadership in Vision, Integrity, Excellence, Teamwork and Accountability & Transparency respectively. UGC directives also places significant premium on the persons proven leadership qualities, administrative capabilities and integrity & morals and less on teaching and research credentials. Actually gone are the days when the search committees were consisting of the distinguished persons known for public service and personal integrity. Neither anyone whatsoever would have dared to seek favours from them nor they would have shown any laxity in trying to search and select the most appropriate person for the post. But unfortunately, now search committees generally consists of the persons who are presumed to be ever ready to profit from this opportunity.

The allegations about the political interference and irregularities in the appointment of Vice Chancellors are getting louder and louder every passing day. Besides, finding more and more Vice Chancellors and registrars embroiled in the cases of corruption and other irregularities, makes amply clear that the rot has badly invaded the universities. There are certainly issues of all sorts which are impairing the selection procedures for the appointment of Vice Chancellors. Persons appointed not on the basis of his or her own merit but by seeking favours, have been found to have either least or no value for merit and more importantly lacks commitment for the greater good of the institution. Such persons have been found to remain busy in taking care of their own interests and of their masters at a cost of institutional interests. A study has found that the lobbying by the professors for administrative positions has resulted in lowering the status of these offices. The autonomy which the universities were enjoying, has got eroded mainly for the reason that these less deserving Vice Chancellors, on the one hand are respected less and on the other hand are lacking courage and the commitment to stand firm to protect the genuine interests of their institutions. In the past, prominent academicians were offered such coveted positions but now the academicians of all hues remains busy in lobbying to seek favours to become Vice Chancellors.

It would be unfair to paint every academician with the same brush. There are very worthy academicians as well but the above-mentioned study conducted by five former Vice Chancellors and 20 Professors has revealed that the procedures being followed for the appointment of Vice Chancellors acts as a disincentive for the worthy academicians who always prefer academic autonomy and self-respect to money and public life. If we want to save these higher learning institutions from further decay, there is an urgency to see that only the most worthy academicians are appointed to the position of Vice Chancellors, otherwise the NEP-2020 which in many ways is path breaking, will fail to deliver the due dividends to the nation. The new policy has talked about the leadership crisis in the HEIs but has nothing concrete to offer to deal with this serious governance issue. Therefore, if we have to set these institutions of great prominence on the track of meaningful growth and development, the Hon. Chancellors would need to immediately attend this pressing and distressing issue. This is the right time to rise above all considerations to save these centres of higher learning with which the dreams and aspirations of future generations are linked.

References

Rohan Prem Kumar, "Vice Chancellors being Prosecuted for Corruption is a blot on Civilisation", *The Hindu*, 20 December 2019.

Indian Society of Bio-informatics, "75% of VCs Unfit to Hold Post: Study", *Times News Network*, 21 February 2019.

14

Appointment of Vice Chancellors in Indian Universities: Calls for a Procedural Rejig

A Vice Chancellor is the executive and academic head of an university, with the responsibility to provide a leadership role, aiming to galvanise everybody in the organisation towards a common goal of achieving excellence in whatever they do. To perform such a critical role, Vice Chancellor requires to be a visionary with a proven track record of outstanding academic leadership and administrative abilities with high moral standards. The Acts governing state or central universities as well as the criterion stipulated by the UGC, defines the selection procedure for such a coveted position. Even though there are well-defined procedures for the appointment of Vice Chancellors, yet the allegations about the political interference and irregularities in the appointment of Vice Chancellors are getting louder and louder every passing day. Besides, finding more and more Vice Chancellors and registrars embroiled in the alleged cases of corruption and other irregularities, makes it amply clear that there seems to exist some rot in the selection process. In order to enable universities to meet the challenges and demands of the 21st century, there is an urgency to identify the rot with which the selection process suffers and what needs to be done to make it fool proof to the extent possible?

The process starts with the constitution of a 'Search Committee' which ordinarily should consist of the distinguished persons of national or international repute with an impeccable track record of honesty and personal integrity. Much, rather everything depends upon the quality of the members of the search committees. Unfortunately, gone are the days when the search committees were consisting of the distinguished persons known for their distinguished public service and personal integrity. Now the search committees generally consists of the persons, who merely by virtue of holding positions of Vice Chancellors, etc. are nominated as members of the search committees rather than for having unblemished character and public prominence. It is widely believed that many of them happen to be Vice Chancellors only due to their political and other connections. Unworthy members have been found ever-ready to profit from this opportunity nationwide. Therefore, the rot mainly lies in the constitution of search committees, which needs to be taken care of otherwise it will worsen the situation beyond any repair.

In the past, only persons of great repute and integrity used to be the members of the search committees. No one whatsoever could have even dared to seek favours from them nor they have ever been found showing any laxity in their efforts to search and select the most appropriate persons for the post. Fortunately, there is no dearth of people of great repute and integrity in the country but unfortunately such people by and large are ignored for such a crucial national duty, generally unwittingly. If the chancellors want to see our universities competing at the global level to feature among the top 100 universities, there is an urgency to see only the most worthy people are getting appointed as Vice Chancellors. The only stepping stone to achieve this noble goal would be constituting search committees consisting of great personalities, giving them freehand to search and select the outstanding and enthusiastic institutional leaders for our universities. Equally important would be that once a search committee is constituted, it is not made to report anybody till the task is finished as per the laid down procedures.

In the past there used to be a 'Search Committee' whose modus operandi was to search a best few, but now there has been a transition from 'Search Committees' to 'Search-cum-Selection Committees' which for all practical purposes are like any other selection committees. This transition raises a million-dollar question, "Is This Transition Good or Bad?" The earlier mechanism of searching the best is more appropriate, with a caveat that the committee members are truly worthy by all standards. However, presently a 'Search-cum-Selection Committee Model' is being followed. But this model is being questioned on the grounds of lack of transparency, and the other limitations with which it suffers. It is being observed that short listing is generally being done without following any scientific methodology. Few typical examples in this regard include; in 2013 the 'Search-cum-Selection' committee constituted for the appointment of Vice Chancellor, Central University of Kashmir shortlisted certain applicants and had even interaction with them. But then with the change in Govt. at Delhi in 2014, the new committee was constituted, which shortlisted different group of applicants from almost the same pool of applicants. Another case in point, the committee for the appointment of Vice Chancellor, Kashmir University in 2018 shortlisted 9 candidates, had interaction with them, however, the panel submitted by the committee reportedly was returned by the then Honourable Chancellor with the direction to readvertise the post. Very recently 'Search-cum-Selection Committee' for Cluster Universities shortlisted none of the candidates from Union Territory of J&K except one from Jammu University. Once there was much hue and cry in local press about the alleged arbitrariness in the short listing of the candidates, the panels of selected candidates for the two universities submitted by the committees were shelved/ rejected by the office of the Chancellor and consequently new committees were constituted. Such a bold move was appreciated by one and all, which made people to believe that wrongdoings no more can be allowed under the current regime. It is an open fact that the members of the committees who generally happen to be academicians, sitting or former Vice Chancellors, have been found quite susceptible to all sorts of pressures, thus ever-ready to compromise, though with some exceptions. "Politicians have used the appointment process to reward their supporters, and Vice Chancellors have increasingly been appointed based on minimum qualifications rather than leadership capacity and vision" (Alya Mishra, 05 Dec. 2010, *University World News*).

The only solution to all this lies in two things—first, that the 'Search-cum-Selection' committees should consist of those persons only who are academicians of great prominence not only in terms of academic excellence but more for having a well-known track record of personal integrity. Second, by evolving a selection process which has in-built objectivity and transparency. The Yash Pal Committee Report on Renovating Higher Education also battled for greater transparency in the selection process. Towards making selection process transparent with greater objectivity, there is a need to decide about the 'Attributes' which the 'Search-cum-Selection' committee would need to consider for short listing and while finalising the panel. UGC has rightly stipulated that an applicant for the post of Vice Chancellor should be a distinguished academician and a Visionary with highest level of Integrity & Morals, Leadership Qualities, Proven Administrative Capabilities, and Outstanding Academic Record. To leave little or no room for personal bias, there is an urgency to make short listing process purely based on objective criterion. For this purpose, out of 1000 points, 75% weightage is proposed to be assigned to the selected academic administrative credentials of the applicants to be considered for short listing and 25% to the interaction with the members of the committee. The following weightage is suggested for different parameters at the stages of screening of applications and interaction with the shortlisted candidates:

S. No.	Parameter	Total Score Assigned
(A)	**At the Stage of Screening**	750
1a	Teaching Experience:	100
	• For every year, 4 points above the mandatory 10 years experience as Professor	20
	• International Teaching Exp.	30
	• Chairs Held	30
	• Visiting Professorship	20

2a	Administrative Experience: • Pro Vice Chancellor • Rectors/Directors of Off-Site campuses • Dean of Deans • Dean of the faculty • HOD • Registrar of a university • Controller of Examinations	**350** 80 60 50 40 30 50 40
3a	Academic Record: • D.Lit./Post Doc. • Fellowships	**50** 30 20
4a	Research Output: • No. of Citations in Public Policy-making Documents • No. of Citations • Funding for Sponsored Research Projects • No. of Books Published • No. of Patents Registered • Consultancy • No. of Newspaper columns on policy documents	**200** **40** 40 40 20 25 25 10
5a	Membership of Apex Decision-making Bodies: • University Council • University Syndicate • University Finance Committee • Member of Academic bodies of other Universities • Member of working groups formed by the Govts.	**50** 10 10 10 10 10
(B)	**At the Stage of Interaction**	**250**
1b	• Vision and Mission • Leadership Philosophy • Presentation	100 100 50

More weightage is proposed to be assigned to the administrative experience for obvious reasons, i.e. the Vice

Chancellor is required to govern the administrative affairs in the most effective manner which in turn calls for having a greater academic administrative exposure. Besides, the success to lead an university to achieve greater heights would mainly depend upon Vice Chancellors vision for the institution and his or her leadership philosophy. These two attributes cannot be measured objectively, thus can be assessed only at the stage of interaction. However, to get a fair idea during the interaction, the candidates need to be given enough time to present their vision/mission for the university and the kind of leadership philosophy he or she will embrace to galvanise everybody to achieve excellence in teaching and research. Video recording of the interaction would add more credibility to the whole process. For the purposes of transparency, the points scored by each candidate at each stage should be made public on the website of the university.

To achieve excellence at par with the international standards, there is an urgency to put distinguished academicians at the helm of affairs of universities. But even if an academic leader is the most distinguished academician but lacking in moral attributes, such leaders have been found to have proved more injurious to the interests of the universities than the leaders who are honest even though less distinguished academicians. It is an established fact that the nations become great not merely due to their natural resources endowments but through morality and inspired vision of their leaders which is more true about the academic institutions. Therefore, ultimately it is the "Honesty and Personal Integrity" of a Vice Chancellor which matters the most. It is only those leaders who are honest with selfless devotion to the greater good of the institution, are trusted and respected the most thus able to galvanise everyone to focus their energies towards the achievement of institutional goals. Therefore, apart from being a visionary with proven track record of leadership and administrative capabilities, a vice-chancellor needs to have a "Leadership in Integrity and Honesty". It would be difficult for the 'Search-cum-Selection' committee members to enquire about the moral attributes of the applicants selected for nomination to Hon. Chancellor. The only solution to such critical issue would be, that the Hon. Chancellor before taking final call on the panel of academicians submitted, involve some investigating agency to secretly and confidentially enquire about their track record of honesty, conduct and other attributes from the organisations where they are working or have worked. This to a great extent will allow to filter dishonest elements from occupying these 'Temples of Knowledge'. If it becomes a nationwide policy then automatically it will create a healthy work culture in the universities.

Reference

Alya Mishra (2010), "India: Crisis of Leadership in Higher Education," University World News, December 5, 2010.

15

Leadership Qualities of Successful Vice Chancellors in the Indian Context

The word university is derived from a Latin word '*universus*' meaning "whole, entire or the whole world." So, university is sort of a world of its own consisting of teachers, scholars, students and others from diverse cultures, races, regions and religious beliefs who interact and question freely to understand, create, and convey. Such an interaction is always aimed to gain & apply knowledge to expand personal growth & opportunity, advance social & community development, foster economic competitiveness, and improve quality of life. This universe is unique in the sense that people here enjoys freedom to question, and to explore with intellectual curiosity and without any prejudice different frontiers of knowledge across socio-economic and other domains of human life. Autonomy to foster creativity for the greater good of all, is the guiding principle on which its governance structures are mainly based. Being the centres of wisdom, people belonging to these universes are presumed to be pure with intellectual curiosity, piety, justice and equity. Given the above stated beautiful and serene landscape, universities are expected to contribute to the universe existing beyond their boundaries in the following respects:

- To develop human resources who are competent to manage socio-economic domains professionally and efficiently in their chosen fields of specialisation with a spirit of social justice.

- To build character, enable learners to be ethical, rational, compassionate, caring with an urge to engage vigorously & fearlessly in the spirit of truth by providing a platform to debate with the purpose to learn and relearn, while at the same time prepare them for gainful employment.
- To innovate new technologies, processes and plausible solutions to the socio-economic problems being faced at the local, national and global level respectively to advance social and community development, foster economic competitiveness, and improve quality of life of people.
- To develop students for leadership in public life by offering an environment which stimulates and nurture their attitudes and interests for assuming leadership roles in public life.

The achievement of these cherished goals requires existence of an enabling ecosystem, the most critical elements of which includes; autonomy to govern free from external interference; a well-articulated 'Institutional Vision'; and dynamic governance structures and systems, consistent with the 'Institutional Vision and Mission' statements. The leadership role of an 'Academic Leader' is all the more important to navigate an university seamlessly to achieve excellence in its stated goals. The criticality of leadership in universities is more pervasive as it acts like a pivot around which rotates the entire edifice. As being cornerstone of an university on which learning communities function and grow, these can make or mar an university. A leader is the one who influences the behaviour of the people around him or her in a manner to inspire them to transcend their self-interests and strive willingly and enthusiastically to achieve organisational goals. Therefore, the pertinent question is, "What leadership qualities a 'Vice Chancellor' who is mainly responsible to offer a leadership role, should possess to be able to carry everybody along to achieve a common goal? To be able to make everybody in the organisation to work tirelessly towards a common goal of achieving excellence, apart from being a noted academician with a strong administrative acumen, a Vice Chancellor needs to possess five leadership qualities like; Leadership in vision, Leadership in integrity, Leadership in excellence, Leadership in accountability and transparency, and Leadership in autonomy and teamwork.

Leadership in Vision/Mission

There is a common saying in management that "No road will lead you to the destination, if you don't know where you are going." This reflects the essence of having a clear vision for the institution that he or she leads. A leader can meet the aspirations of the people only when he or she is a visionary. A visionary leader is one who is able to gauge the potential of his nation or institution and at the same time has a clear idea of how to get there. Therefore, to achieve excellence in whatever an university does, a Vice Chancellor needs to be a visionary with great passion i.e. has to have a very clear and realistic description of what an university would like to achieve in the future. He or she will be able to have well-crafted vision for the university only when he "Thinks Globally and Acts Locally" which calls for having an exposure to the world class universities. Along with the plausible vision, Vice Chancellor needs to have a well-articulated mission in mind, delineating the blueprint of the strategies and the processes necessary to achieve the milestones specified in the institutional vision. However, it will be highly critical for the Vice Chancellor to demonstrate energy and total commitment to the vision and mission continuously and visibly this calls for having a strong passion for the institutional vision. Equally important for the Vice Chancellor will be to take all the requisite steps to foster values throughout the university consistent with the vision and mission. It is an established fact that "visionary leadership is rare and certainly not something an average person can have it" (Suzanne Lucas). It is in view of this fact that it is being forcefully argued that while searching persons for vice chancellorship, it should be seen whether he or she is a 'Visionary'.

Leadership in Accountability and Transparency

Successful leaders are anti status quo, thus creative and innovative. To achieve excellence, creative leaders take initiatives often involving calculated risks while considering the common good. But what makes them to inspire and make everybody to rally in support of new initiatives, the leader takes the responsibility and ownership for decisions, actions and results. Besides, they believe in greater transparency in whatever they do which leaves no room for people in the organisation to unnecessarily attach ulterior motives, rather helps to earn trust and confidence of everybody in the organisation. It is not only the Vice Chancellor taking responsibility for decisions but all in the university need to be made accountable for their expected roles. This calls for putting in place "Institutional Effectiveness Mechanism" which according to SACSCOC Resource Manual, is a systematic, explicit, and documented process of measuring performance against the mission in all aspects of an institution." Equally important for the leadership in accountability is to create an environment in the organisation where criticism is not muzzled on the pretext of being an unnecessary opposition rather takes it positively as an input to improve further. In the western universities, Vice Chancellors themselves constitute an "Adversarial Committees" with a mandate to periodically present their critique of the policies and programmes initiated to improve results. This helps on the one hand, to plug the gaps if any left while framing policies and programmes and on the other hand, results in greater synergy and cohesiveness in the organisation.

Leadership in Excellence

It implies that an academic leader should strive for excellence in everything they do by continuously cultivating 'Intellectual, Physical and Spiritual' culture throughout the organisation. This is possible only when an academic leader places premium only on merit, performance and personal integrity rather than on personal relations. Vice chancellors with leadership in excellence, leaves no scope for favouritism, nepotism and personal likings and dislikings rather makes 'Merit, Merit and Merit' only his or her mantra in governance. Such a situation in an organisation makes everyone to believe that to earn positions/promotions, one would need to invest their time and energies in achieving excellence in their respective domains rather in wasting time in cultivating relationships to seek favours, thus promotes healthy work culture. It is a well-established fact, that such organisations fail to perform well where merit and personal integrity is being compromised to favour some sycophants who are mostly mediocre, lacking integrity and commitment to the institution thus eats the very vitals required for achieving excellence. This results into a culture of sycophancy rather than gaining currency for performance, credibility and commitment to the cause of institutional growth and development. Weak leaders generally create coterie of 'Yes Man' who are ever ready to compromise regardless of the consequences on the institution.

Leadership in Teamwork

Steve Jobs has changed the whole complexion of human living with his invention but equally the credit goes to his team of highly motivated professionals who worked with zeal and zest to translate his dream into a reality. Teamwork is essential to achieve organisational goals as it motivates unity in the workplace, offers differing perspectives & feedback, offers greater learning opportunities and promotes workplace synergy. Therefore, to be successful, an academic leader has to work cooperatively as a member of a team and remains deeply committed to the overall team/institutional goals rather than own interests. The leaders who believes in teamwork, values & respects all campus constituents, celebrate diversity, and embrace shared governance by fostering inclusiveness in decision-making. "You are not real leader unless people follow you voluntarily and for that to happen, your team members need to feel heard out and listened to you" (Suzanne Lucas, 2021). Teamwork also enables management to 'Sell the Changes' successfully throughout the organisation, thus enables to initiate radical changes in the system without any resistance. A leader who lacks team spirit has generally been found to have failed to enthuse others to work together to achieve milestones. Universities in India are autonomous bodies with inbuilt democratic governance structures. But unfortunately, over a period of time, there has been greater erosion in the autonomy of universities, more so in state universities, both within and from outside which has done a great damage to the culture of 'Participative Decision-Making' with a serious fallout on the institutional efficiency.

Leadership in Integrity

The pivot around which all the above stated core values of academic leadership rotates is the 'Leadership in Honesty and Personal Integrity' of a leader. It is an established fact that the nations become great not merely due to their natural resources endowments but through morality and inspired vision of their leaders which is more true about the academic institutions. Therefore, ultimately it is the "Honesty and Personal Integrity" of a Vice Chancellor which matters the most. Only the visionary leaders with impeccable track record of honesty and integrity, are able to influence the behaviour of the people around him to strive willingly and enthusiastically to achieve organisational goals. To be honest is important but more important is to appear to be honest as we all know that actions speak louder than words. Thus to galvanise everybody in the organisation, an academic leader needs to demonstrate honesty and ethical behaviour in all spheres of administration. It is only those leaders who are honest with selfless devotion to the greater good of the institution, are trusted and respected the most, thus able to galvanise everyone to focus their energies towards the achievement of institutional goals.

Final Word

Only genuinely distinguished academicians are seen to possess the above stated interconnected leadership qualities which are highly essential to navigate academic institutions towards achieving excellence in whatever they do. Such great academicians are generally having selfless devotion to the institutional goals. In the past, prominent academicians were offered such coveted positions but now the academicians of all hues remains busy in lobbying to seek favours to become Vice Chancellors. Those academicians who are desperate to become Vice Chancellors and use all means in their command for the purpose, generally lacks the above essential leadership qualities. Their goal from day one remains how they can remain glued to the chair. Besides, their nature of management, generally does not correspond with their role profiles, thus fails to make any noticeable mark either on the institution or any stakeholder whatsoever. The organisations under their command are administered more than strategically managed. Their culture is one of *Bureaucratic Maze* than that of creative and innovative leaders with a well-crafted vision and mission for the university.

Reference

Suzanne Lucas (2021), "Visionary Leadership has 3 Characteristics You Want to Find and Follow," *The Balance Careers*, September 27, 2021 (https://www.thebalancecareers.com)

16

Planning and Assessing Institutional Effectiveness: Panacea for all Ills in Higher Education in India

It has become quite fashionable for higher educational institutions (HEIs) in the country to have a well-crafted vision and mission statements. It is good, rather quite essential to have a very realistic vision and mission as it enables institutions to define the processes and strategies needed to achieve their goals. Vision is aspirational in nature in the sense that it describes the futuristic aspirations of an institution. It constantly keeps reminding everyone in the organization where they want to be in future. Whereas, mission is a purpose statement of an organisation and describes what processes and operational strategies are needed to achieve the envisioned milestones. But unfortunately HEIs by and large have failed to translate their vision and mission statements into reality by using them as a guiding philosophy for achieving their intended goals. The vision and mission statements are not merely to be printed in official publications or displayed on the walls of the institution but these need to be used as a means to seek continuous improvements in institutional performance. By doing so, it defeats the very essence of having a vision and mission for the institution which otherwise are aimed to plan and control performances at all levels in the organisation by defining answers to the following pertinent questions:

- What kind of goals do we want to achieve?
- When are we going to achieve the intended goals?
- How are we going to achieve our short-term and long-term goals?

As per the requirements of National Assessment and Accreditation Council (NAAC), universities in the country have established full-fledged Directorates of Internal Quality Assurance (DIQA) with a mandate to assure quality educational pursuits. But unfortunately, DIQAs by and large have misconstrued their roles to the extent of either publishing annual reports or the conduct of "Evaluation of Teaching" by the students that too for fulfilling the requirements of NAAC accreditation process rather than for seeking improvements in teaching. These directorates of great significance generally comes into action only when accreditation of a university by NAAC is near the corner. To realise the milestones specified in the institutional vision in today's complex and dynamic environment largely depends upon effective 'Performance Planning and Control Systems'. Organizations which have proper performance management systems in place, are more than twice as successful as similar organizations (Phadnis, 2002). But unfortunately, HEIs in India are largely operating in a vacuum i.e. without tracking the performances of individual faculty members and departments/centres based on 'Peer Benchmarking or Best Practices Approach'. As such, the huge public funding that goes into HEIs largely fails to yield due dividends. In fact, the failure to govern in a systematic manner is being considered one of the prominent reasons for HEIs to have failed to perform well. Until and unless our HEIs lays due emphasis on the management of institutional effectiveness like their counterparts in the western world, we will fail to capitalise the potential with which our institutions are endowed. Some HEIs have started to audit academics but unfortunately in an unplanned manner which is sure to fail to make any headway in the academics rather will undermine its utility once for all. This sadly reflects intellectual/professional bankruptcy of such institutions which otherwise are expected to help and guide other institutions in effective governance by offering improved systems and solutions.

The fact of the matter is that the DIQAs have a significant role to play in seeking continuous improvements in academics and other related pursuits in line with the stated vision and mission statements of the universities. This calls for the DIQAs to operate a system of "Institutional Effectiveness Mechanism" to provide leadership, guidance and support to each unit in the university by planning, assessing, analysing, and reporting processes that contribute to the achievement of university goals. One of the most prominent best practices of HEIs in the western world has been making "Institutional Effectiveness Mechanism" an integral part of the governance system to foster continuous improvements in academics. According to SACSCOC Resource Manual, "Institutional Effectiveness is a systematic, explicit, and documented process of measuring performance against the mission in all aspects of an institution." It is a whole process of aligning departmental vision and mission statements with that of an institution; in line with the goals, set performance targets for each faculty member, department/centre, school, and student support centres; measure actual performances and compare the same with the standard performance to find out variations if any and propose corrective actions to be taken to plug the gaps in targeted performances.

The first step in the implementation of "Institutional Effectiveness Mechanism" is to establish long term "Institutional Strategic Plan," the duration of which may vary from institution to institution, depending upon the constraints of visibility and milestones to be accomplished. NEP-2020 has also recommended that each HEIs will have to make a strategic 'Institutional Development Plan' (IDP) on the basis of which institutions will develop initiatives, assess their own progress, and reach the goals set therein, which could then become the basis for further public funding. A "Strategic Planning Committee" will need to be constituted for framing a 'Strategic Plan', mainly consisting of few Subject Experts' Selected Administrators & Deans and Student representatives. Given the interconnectedness of the 'Institutional Strategic Plan' with those of teaching departments, schools, and student support service centres, while framing plans, the strategic committee is required to use "Top-down & Bottom-up Approach" which calls for prioritisation of strategic processes and programmes at all levels in the university. However, to align and realign the planning process successfully, among other things, the strategic committee would require to have ongoing dialogue and feedback from all departments/schools/ centres. These inclusive discussions are based on "Living Plan Philosophy", where the reliable information and insights are available to the 'Strategic Committee' to make informed decisions about new initiatives.

The 'Strategic Plan,' at the institutional and other levels in a university shall have to be based on 'Vision and Mission Statements', therefore, to ensure very effective planning at all levels in a university, such statements need to be very realistic. But the fact is that many of the HEIs in the country formulate their vision and mission statements just for the sake of formality, thus generally are not realistic, plausible and specific. Therefore, the first step while establishing 'Institutional Strategic Plan' would be to rewrite the institutional vision and mission statements in a manner that reflects the achievements that can be accomplished. Equally important would be to align the vision and mission statements of all the departments, schools and student support centres with that of the institution. However, the vision and mission statements should clearly reflect their core activities with measurable goals.

The second step in the implementation of "Institutional Effectiveness Mechanism" is to decide about the intended outcomes for the core activities for each Dept./school/centre to act as 'Standards of Efficiency'. At a teaching department level, the intended outcomes are required to be set at the level of individual faculty members and for the department as a whole. At the level of individual faculty member, for Teaching Performance; Research Output; and Participation in Conferences, Seminars, & Workshops, intended outcomes need to be set, while as at the departmental level, outcomes need to be set about the Quality of Academic and Research Programmes; Quality of Course Curriculum; Teaching-Learning Environment; Implementation of Academic Calendar; Co-Curricular Activities; Placements and Extension & Outreach Activities. It would be highly essential that the outcomes need to concentrate only on key areas. Most critical would be that the outcomes are consistent with the vision and mission statements & overall goal of a department/centre and are set after debate and discussion with the concerned. It is also essential to avoid setting too many performance goals, only critical measures should be used to control performances. By doing so, making continuous improvements will receive impetus from the enthusiastic support of all in the organization.

The establishment of indented outcomes proceeds with the measurement of actual performance of each faculty member, and Dept./school/centre, generally on yearly basis. Multiple measurement methods are necessary to assure reliability and validity of the data, however, direct methods are preferred to measure the performances. Wherever, actual data cannot be measured quantitative, Likert Type Scale should be used to convert a qualitative phenomenon into quantitative. Apart from other sources, surveys like Evaluation of Teaching by the Students, Course Objective Survey, Peers Evaluation, Self-Evaluation, Graduating Student Survey, Campus Survey, Parental-Perception Survey, Employers Survey, Exit Survey, Alumni Survey, Student/Faculty Survey of Administration can be employed to generate data to assess different parameters of performances. So key in the generation of data will greatly depend upon how well the instruments for these surveys have been designed and administered to the respondents.

Once the actual data has been collected, the next step is to find out the variations in performances by comparing actual accomplishments with standard outcomes. Before preparing a 'Reports of Required Actions,' all variations whether positive or negative are discussed in detail with the parties concerned to arrive at meaningful conclusions. To foster continuous improvements in the performances, everything will depend upon the 'Reports of Required Actions,' prepared which provides a complete blueprint of actions needed to be taken to plug the gaps in performances. Therefore, all the care will be required to be taken to devise 'Reports of Required Actions,' which should be feasible in terms of time and resources available. The 'Reports of Required Actions,' generally includes corrective actions which may include, infusion of further resources, reorientation of existing processes and strategies, or at times management reshuffle and recognition of excellence by awarding and rewarding the best performers.

In addition to "Strategic Planning Committee", the successful implementation of institutional effectiveness mechanism requires to constitute "Institutional Effectiveness Committee" whose sole responsibility will be to decide about the measurement methods to be used to generate and collect data, design instruments for data collection, collect and analyse data to find variations if any in the institutional effectiveness. The "Institutional Effectiveness Committee" should mainly consist of Director DIQA, Deputy Director DIQA, and Accreditation Liaison Officers. The assessment reports prepared by the effectiveness committee based on the comparison between actual performances and expected performances will have to be reported to the 'Institutional Strategic Planning Committee'. It will be the responsibility of this committee to debate and discuss assessment reports with the concerned Departments/Schools/Centres and to decide about the 'Reports of Required Actions'. Feedback to each unit/person about their scorecard performances delivers both a reading on current headway and message about future expectations. Thus, it is highly desirable to report the headway on each performance parameter with necessary recommendations for realignment of future actions.

The "Institutional Effectiveness Mechanism" is surely a panacea for all the ills which impedes the achievement of excellence in contemporary HEIs as it helps in getting all crevices ironed out. Among other things, it enables to translate vision and mission statements into strategic plans and measurable goals, planning and assessing performance at all levels, evidence-based decision-making, efficient resource allocation, and supports accreditation activities and requirements. Most notable outcome of institutional effectiveness mechanism is that it ensures greater transparency and accountability, which in turn results into a competitive work culture throughout the organisation. Since it makes everybody in the organisation accountable for whatever they do, therefore, there is every possibility that people may resist this changing work environment. Generally, organisations fail to incorporate new systems of governance successfully because of the resistance from the employees for one simple reason that it may push them out of comfort zones. It would be unwise to push the change without seeking clear understanding of everybody about its usefulness both to the organisation and its people. Sometimes new systems fail to yield desired results due to the failure of the management to plan and organise its implementation seamlessly, because the team responsible to manage the new system struggle with the change itself for not having understood the essence of the new system. Stephen Covey Says, "Begin with the end in mind i.e. starting with an objective statement is a wonderful way to understand what processes you are trying to establish, how you are going to go about it, and what results you are trying to achieve." At the top of everything, the commitment of top management which they will have to demonstrate visibly and consistently, would be key to the success of the new system.

Reference

Mary Clotilda (2019), "Everything you need to know about Institutional Effectiveness," *Creatrix Campus*, creatrixcampus.com

17

Evaluation of Teaching by Students: A Controversial Issue in Higher Education in India

Achieving leadership in chosen areas of teaching, research and extension by delivering superior value to all its constituencies, and applying all the times highest professional and ethical standards is generally the vision of the universities operating in the contemporary world settings. To achieve this vision, Academic Leaders/Administrators would need to constantly seek answers to the following questions:

- How are we going to meet the aspirations of our students, potential employers, and society in general?
- What kind of internal elements like curriculum, teaching-learning environment, infrastructural & learning resources etc. are critical to develop students, delight parents, deliver capable and competent brains to employers and to diagnose socio-economic problems confronting economies and the society.

The bottom line for all the above lies in 'Learning and Growth', and to achieve the same, it requires to continually ask ourselves a question "Are We Maintaining Our Ability to Change and Improve?" This calls for having an 'Institutional Effectiveness Mechanism' in place which is a systematic, explicit, and documented process of measuring performance against the vision/mission in all aspects of an institution. One such aspect is the assessment of quality of teaching by the students. In view of NAAC requirement, evaluation of teaching has become a regular feature in universities in the country. But this has been a controversial subject among the teaching community. There are arguments for and against the evaluation of teaching by the students. It is in view of this fact that the universities generally conduct evaluation of teaching by the students on regular basis just to meet the requirement set by NAAC for accreditation rather than using it as a means to foster improvements in the teaching-learning process. However, the only purpose of NAAC to require universities to have a robust evaluation mechanism of teaching by the students is to use it for seeking improvements in teaching-learning process. In the western world, evaluation of teaching by the students is an integral part of the governance in the colleges and universities.

Evaluation of teaching is simply a means to seek feedback from the students about the quality of teaching but there are some in the teaching fraternity who question its authenticity while others raise questions about the ability and bias on the part of students. It is being argued by many that the students lack maturity and the ability to judge the performance of their teachers very reliably. The bias of the students is also being reasoned out for unreliable judgment of the students. It is also being claimed that it is being misused by students by giving high rating to those who give good grades and low rating to those who are very strict, disciplinarians, and who teach thoroughly & give grades purely on the basis of their performances. Gender of the teachers is also claimed to influence the rating of teachers by students. Research has revealed that the teachers physical appearance, gender and age are also found to have affected rating of teaching by students (Buck and Tiene, 1989; Sohar Preston et al., 2016). Younger faculty members were found to receive higher rating (Borint et al., 2016) while more senior faculty received lower ratings (Clayson, 1999). Sometimes students look for easy teachers to pass a subject (Felton et al., 2004), however, research has shown that most of the students tend to search for competent teachers (Feldman, 1984) and credible faculty members (Patton, 1999), thus these findings disapproves the fallacy that easy teachers receive higher ratings. Students frankly praises instructors for their friendly humorous manner in the classroom but if their teaching is not well organised and stimulating for effective learning, students equally frankly criticised them in those areas (Aleamoni, 1981).

Research evidence on the authenticity of evaluation of teaching by the students is conflicting. There may be some merit in the objections raised against the reliability of the evaluation, as such these apprehensions cannot be rejected altogether. But the other side of the story is that since the core function of HEIs remains teaching and learning, therefore, to perform this core activity, it becomes all the more important to assess the quality of teaching. The only way to assess the quality of teaching is by evaluating its effectiveness and the only source to such a useful information are students as they being the real recipients of knowledge who experience the conduct of a teacher, his or her motivation and ability to transfer the knowledge and the extent of knowledge he or she possesses. It is actually a very useful source of feedback from students to the teacher about his teaching etc. thus helps to synergise the teacher-learning process to achieve better learning of students. It also ensures greater accountability in the system with a net outcome of improved teaching. But to minimise the possibility of its misuse by students and to ensure its reliability and validity, it will be all the more important to take every care in the designing of instrument for data collection; procedures used for its administration, tools and techniques used to analyse the data and the way the final results are interpreted and reported.

Much depends on how well the instrument for data collection has been designed. Unfortunately, it has been observed that in our set-up not much attention is being given to the process of designing an instrument. It is the job of an expert but surprisingly amateurs have been found involved to perform this crucial job. If one makes an analysis of the instruments that are in use in our universities, it becomes amply clear that the instruments are deficient in many respects. For example, it does not become clear what kind of attributes of a teachers are being attempted to be assessed. It is also found that the statements in the instrument either does not clearly signify the attribute for which intended or are dichotomous. Besides, the questions/statements are found not being formulated in a manner that are easy to understand, free from information bias, and appropriate to the level of education. To quantify the qualitative phenomena, Likert type scale is being generally used, but surprisingly without any benchmarking of the final results which renders the whole process meaningless.

Keeping in view the central role of the instrument in truly assessing the effectiveness of teaching, due care needs to be given in designing an instrument. Towards this goal, the first step should be to know what are the specific objectives of the assessment. The assessment of teaching effectiveness generally aims to assess 'The Teacher' i.e. his attitude and enthusiasm, and subject knowledge; 'The Teaching Process and Ability'; and Learning Outcomes. Therefore, the instrument should contain the statements measuring the effectiveness of these aspects. A good questionnaire is one which is organised and worded in a manner that encourages respondents to provide accurate, unbiased and complete information. Besides questions/statements should be worded in a manner that are easily understood, and prompts students to answer. Once the instrument has been designed, its reliability and validity needs to be properly checked. Therefore, it is not everybody's domain but a job of specialists only. Number of well-designed instruments are readily available, therefore, it would be more appropriate to adopt the one which suits to ones requirements whose reliability and validity already stands tested.

Procedures for the administration of the instrument and the interpretation of final results are equally important to achieve the intended outcomes of the evaluation. Presently, it is the DIQA which conducts the survey and analysis's the data which is then communicated to the School Deans for its communication to the concerned faculty members. It is a highly sensitive exercise as the honour and dignity of faculty members is directly connected to it, therefore, due care need to be taken to ensure confidentiality. Now online evaluation is being used, therefore, the logistics needed are minimal, as such it would be quite manageable for the offices of School Deans to handle the whole process. But it would be essential for the Deans to keep records pertaining to the assessment in the personal custody for the reasons of confidentiality. Besides, it would be highly appropriate to conduct assessment at the end of each semester, course-wise rather than at the end of the year, not course-wise as the practice goes currently.

The most serious flaw with the current process is that there is no benchmarking of the final scores to conclude about the satisfactory or unsatisfactory performance which in turn renders the whole process meaningless. Generally on five point Likert Type Scale, a score of 3 and above is considered satisfactory which contrarily means a score of less than 3 is considered unsatisfactory. But it is widely accepted that the minimum benchmark for satisfactory performance depends upon the size of a class. In a class of 15-25, 25-40 and 40 & above 80%, 70% and 60% score respectively on a five point scale is considered satisfactory. Besides, there is a need to have a detailed interpretation of the final scores by differentiating the performance on the basis of score intervals into Outstanding, Excellent, Quite Satisfactory, Satisfactory, Unsatisfactory, Quite Unsatisfactory, Poor and Very Poor. Such interpretation is needed to precisely differentiate performances so as to clearly communicate to teachers where they stands. Without such communication, the purpose of conducting the much controversial evaluation will fail to serve the purposes fully. Given the inherent risks in the evaluation, it should be used to seek improvements in the performance of faculty members. Therefore teachers with:

- Outstanding and excellent performance should be applauded by giving a "Certificate of Appreciation";
- Quite satisfactory and satisfactory performance should be appreciated but reminded of making an effort to improve to the next higher grade/level;
- Unsatisfactory and poor performers' should be called by the Dean to guide and advise them for making improvements confidentiality, however, at the same time, they should be cautioned to improve to avoid getting listed in the 'Grey List' or loose annual increments or promotion to the next higher level;
- Poor and very poor performers should be removed from the responsibility of teaching and send to attend faculty development programmes or least given a limited time

period to improve with stoppage of annual increments and promotions to the next higher level until they improve, however, before making any such prescription, it would be highly needed that such faculty members be given an opportunity to explain their position.

Final Word

There is no doubt about certain inherent risks involved in the evaluation of teaching by the students as stated above, but the hard reality is that there is no other alternative to this much needed feedback system. So contemporary higher educational institutions will have to embrace this system to improve quality of teaching but take all the necessary steps to try to keep the risks associated with this system under control. Towards this goal, only those students should be allowed to participate in the evaluation process who have 75% or above attendance. It is also that the evaluation results should be used in conjunction with the peers evaluation and self-evaluation. Added to it, the final conclusions about the performance of a teacher should not be merely based on the results of a single evaluation but on the basis of a series of evaluations, a maximum of three. Besides, while analysing the data, each aspect of a teacher should be thoroughly and scientifically analysed. Like in the rest of the world, not only average score obtained along with standard deviation should be communicated but both, the average score and the scores of each question asked in the questionnaire should be communicated. This will enable faculty members to know in which aspect he or she is doing well or badly, which in turn will enable the teacher to focus on weaker aspects for making improvements. The widely acknowledged recommendation has been that the teacher himself or herself should proactively seek feedback informally to know whether the teaching and learning synergises well so to make timely adjustments to seek better results.

References

Aleamoni, Lawrence M., (1981), "Student Ratings of Institution," *Handbook of Teacher Evaluation*, Edited by Jason Millman, Beverly Hills, CA, Sage Publications.

Buck, S. and Tiene, D. (1989), "The Impact of Physical Attractiveness, Gender, and Teaching Philosophy on Teacher Evaluations," Vol. 82, No. 3, pp. 172-77.

Boring, A., Ottoboni, K. and Stark, P.B. (2016), "Students Evaluation of Teaching (mostly) do not measure Teaching Effectiveness," Science Open Research.

Chayson, D.E. (1999), "Students Evaluation of Teaching Effectiveness: Some Implications of Stability," *Journal of Marketing Education*, Vol. 21, No. 1, pp. 68-75.

Feldman, K.A. (1984), "Class Size and College Students, Evaluation of Teachers and Courses: A Closer Look, *Research in Higher Education*, Vol. 21, No. 1, pp. 45-116.

Felton, J., Mitchell, J. and Stinson, M. (2004), "Web-based Student Evaluation of Professors: The Relations between Perceived Quality. Easiners and Sexiners," Assessment and Evaluation in Higher Education, Vol. 29, No. 1, pp. 91-108.

Patton, T.O. (1999), "Ethnicity and Gender: An Examination of its Impact on Instructor Credibility in the University Classroom," *The Howard Journal of Communications*, Vol. 10, No. 2, pp. 123-44.

Sohr-Preston, S.L., Bowell, S.S., McCaleb K. and Robertson, D. (2016), "Professor Gender, Age and Hotness in Influencing College Students' Generation and Interpretation of Professors Rating," *Higher Learning Research Communications*, Vol. 6, No. 3, pp. 1-23.

18

Integrating Formative, Continuous and Comprehensive Assessment System into Higher Education

New education policy 2020 has comprehensively covered the entire gamut of education and has offered important amendments and transformational reforms both in school education and higher education. The new policy aims to overcome the flaws with which the education system in the country is confronted and also to meet the demands of 21st century. At the higher educational level, new policy offers whole gamut of reforms towards multidisciplinary system of education, reorganisation of regulatory systems, transformation of institutional structures, institutional autonomy, reimagining the vocational education, teacher education, enabling learning environment, etc. But towards an equally important aspect of education i.e. teaching pedagogy and assessment it makes a mere mention of granting greater autonomy to the faculty in framing teaching pedagogy and assessment. Nothing significant has been recommended in the policy document about the current state of examination and the reforms needed to make assessment more result oriented.

It is known to one and all that everything is not well with the current system of examination at the higher education level. We largely continue with the age-old examination system which remains heavily weighted in favour of summative semester/year-end written external examination as such, suffers from some serious limitations. It is not considered a valid and reliable measure of students cognitive, and affective abilities. It is also widely seen as a test of memory, thus fails to encourage and assess higher order abilities and other qualities. Besides, examination in the current form induces anxiety and has come to mean stress and strain thereby renders learning process boring rather than enjoyable. The most serious drawback with the current system of examination is that it is punitive in nature rather than diagnostic, remedial and improvement based in nature as it fails to provide credible feedback to the learners right in time to take remedial measures. At the top of all these serious drawbacks, it does not allow learner to gain dynamic knowledge by allowing students to actively participate in the process of learning and knowledge creation.

Though faculty enjoys autonomy to evolve best practices in teaching pedagogy and assessment yet, it is sad to state that we have collectively failed to change with the changing situations. Unfortunately, we continue to use the age-old teaching pedagogy and assessment. Our assessment system continues to remain heavily weighted towards summative semester-end written examination. It is heavily oriented towards textbook knowledge rather than aiming to seek development of the overall personality. The assessment methods must be scientific, designed to continuously improve learning and test the application of knowledge. The panacea for all these ills lies only in the "Proactive Teaching-Learning System", the essential features of which includes; continuous and comprehensive evaluation, and learning outcomes based assessment. Under this proactive system, the assessment is not done at the end of a semester rather continuously by employing diverse assessment methods like class tests, presentations, case studies, games, role playing, project work and assignments. Proactive system allows outcome-based assessment thus allows learners to achieve practical and dynamic knowledge. Realising these and other flaws with the existing system of examination, a continuous formative assessment system has also been recommended in NEP-2020.

Continuous and comprehensive formative assessment system not only allows to assess the subject knowledge but also measures and helps to build and improve life skills (co-scholastic) such as; social, emotional and communication skills and critical thinking. Besides, the teacher-made tests used under proactive system are conducted in a relatively informal and non-threatening atmosphere thus are considered to have high pedagogical value. It is also that the focus is not entirely on the assessment for formal certification but more to achieve the overall growth and development of a student by continuously assessing the progress of the learners so as to provide them feedback for making improvements. As already stated that by nature it is diagnostic and remèdial rather than punitive like the summative system of assessment. Proactive system of education is based on a fundamental premise that the classrooms are not homogeneous rather heterogeneous, presuming that some students are very bright and very much interested in their studies; some have basic intellect but require some pushing by the teachers; and some are below average or have less interest in studies, thus require greater focus or pushing from the teachers. Under proactive system, students are assessed continuously to identify particularly the last group so as to have greater focus on them with a purpose to make them to improve their learning.

Unfortunately our current system of examination involves using same pattern and type of question papers across all disciplines. It is quite illogical to have a same type of question paper across all streams, disciplines and subjects when most of these are quite different to each other. The assessment methods are actually guided by the learning outcomes, therefore, are but natural to vary from discipline to discipline and even subject to subject. Besides, format of question papers used currently aims to assess academic knowledge only. Therefore, it generally promotes rote learning which in turn renders the assessment less meaning in today's demanding and complex landscape of education. It is in view of this fact that the performance awarded under the existing system lacks confidence of the end users like employers, and even of the higher learning institutions which while making admissions for higher studies conduct admission tests rather than making admission on the marks awarded by the same university. It is also that the existing format which generally consists of very short, short and long-answer questions, limits the flexibility to test higher-order abilities. These are generally designed to test a detailed knowledge of the textbook rather than competencies, application, Analysis & Synthesis of knowledge. Added to it, there is a greater possibility of the repetition of identical or very similar questions year after year, hence playing in the hands of pseudo-coaching centres. Under the proactive system of education, the continuous & comprehensive assessment methods solves most of these issues. Since it is mainly teacher-centered system, the format of question paper under this system is based on learning outcomes, therefore, varies from discipline to discipline and even within discipline, from subject to subject. Since being not only continuous but also comprehensive, therefore generally teachers use a combination of assessment methods like, class test, project work, presentations, case studies, etc. depending upon the nature of the subject. As such allows to assess dynamic & practical knowledge and life skills thus higher order abilities. The semester-end examination is generally theoretical but mainly contains practice-oriented questions which allows even open book examination.

Conduct and evaluation under the current summative semester-end examination system is largely centralised and third-party paid-up job. Given the number of students at the undergraduate level, arranging logistics for conducting examination by a centralised agency becomes quite formidable, complex and difficult job. Equally evaluation of answer scripts becomes a daunting job due to the largeness and subjective nature of answer scripts which in turn has adversely impacted the quality of evaluation which is evident from the large number of complaints and grade appeals. Besides, it is time consuming and a very expensive affair. Other than the establishment costs, on an average University of Kashmir bears an expenditure of around ₹ 8-9 Crores annually in the conduct of examinations. Proactive system of education provides solution to all these problems. Under this system, in addition to comprehensive continuous assessment, there is a scope for semester-end examination which is scheduled centrally but the whole process is arranged and managed by the concerned teachers who if requires are provided with the invigilating staff by a central agency. Therefore, being a teacher-centered system, one it does not become a daunting job for anybody whatsoever and second it consumes less time and is least expensive as conducting the whole process of the examination is considered as a part of the job of a teacher. Open book examination and online proctored examination are some of the modes used to conduct class tests and semester-end examinations. Under the system, the examination results are declared both informally by the teachers concerned on the very first day of the new semester and later on formally by the central agency.

The current summative semester-end written examination also lacks transparency and accountability, thus resulting into more complaints and more grade appeals. At the same time, making a grade appeal costs to a student irrespectively of the fact that he or she has every right to see whether marking has been done fairly or not. Besides, being centralised, grade appeal system is time consuming and a costly affair for the students as a result suffers from poor student satisfaction. It is an open fact that there are always question marks on the quality of question papers which at least is evident from the percentage of questions that are usually found either wrong or out of syllabus or with wrong choices of answers with respect to the admission test papers. My personal experience has been that many a times we come across with poor quality question papers, mainly downloaded from the internet. Contrary to the summative semester-end written examination, 'Transparency and Accountability' is the hallmark of this proactive system of education. Under this system, on the very first day of a new semester, the teacher has to return answer copies to the students to fulfil his or her right to see whether the answers have been awarded marks fairly or not. A student has a right to question his teacher then and there about the marking if he or she feels to have not been given due marks. After having explained by a teacher, if still a student is not satisfied, he or she is allowed to make a grade appeal to a Dean of the School on prescribed format readily available on the official website free of any charge. Upon receiving the grade appeal, generally the Dean gets the paper re-evaluated in his presence by two subject experts and the average of the two evaluators is taken as final. Besides, students are within their rights to cross check with the answer copies of any other student which very rarely happens because of greater accountability in the system. This system of transparency and accountability on the one hand results into greater confidence and student satisfaction and on the other hand into greater accountability of the teachers, the net outcome from all this is greater efficiency both from the side of students and the faculty.

Continuous and comprehensive assessment system has a risk of misuse by students and faculty. While giving assignments, there is every probability that a student may resort to plagiarism which can be easily ascertained by the anti-plagiarism software's which are readily available in almost all the institutions. Besides, this problem to a great extent can also be taken care of by giving research-based projects, case studies, role playing, internship projects and presentations. In business management subjects, even business games are used to enable the students to practice knowledge in a simulated environment. Equally important risk to this teacher-centered system may emanate from the teacher itself. There is every possibility more so in our ecosystem that the teacher may not be very particular about the quality of assessment process or may fail to maintain competitiveness of the system. But given this potential risk, the solution is not to reject this useful system on this pretext but to put adequate checks and balances in place. Partly this system has been in operation at the post-graduate level but needs to be fully embraced in the interest of better teaching-learning outcomes. NEP-2020 has already recommended a greater autonomy to the teachers to allow them to be innovative and creative in designing the course curriculum, teaching pedagogy, and assessment. Besides the new policy has recommended a continuous formative assessment system to be used. Eventually, the recommendation of NEP-2020 to convert affiliating degree colleges as autonomous degree granting college, will allow colleges to be the examining bodies of their own students which again will pave way for teacher-centered continuous and comprehensive assessment system. At the top of all these arguments, we need to have a confidence in the integrity of our teachers who surely are worthy to adopt all the progressive changes with a caveat that the academic leaders demonstrate leadership in teamwork, accountability, transparency, excellence and personal integrity and honesty.

SECTION FOUR

Reforming Assessment and Accreditation Process

- Quality Assurance in Indian Higher Education
- Assessment and Accreditation of Higher Education: Calls for Refinements of Key Indicators of Quality Parameters

19

Quality Assurance in Indian Higher Education

Achieving excellence in teaching and research is the goal of every higher education institution (HEI), the world over. To achieve excellence, HEIs would need to have a greater focus on the quality of its teaching and research pursuits. Therefore, the sole objective of the HEIs and their regulators is to continuously make efforts to improve the quality of higher education. HEIs keep on building capacities in terms of quality infrastructure, committed and highly qualified human resources and processes and programmes to harness the potential necessary to ensure better quality in their pursuits. HEIs also keep on reviewing its policies and programmes periodically so as to evolve to meet the changing requirements of the knowledge economy. However, the greater responsibility for ensuring quality teaching and research in higher education lies on the regulators, particularly the Accrediting Institutions. On the recommendations of NEP-1986 and the Programme of Action (POA), National Assessment and Accreditation Council (NAAC) was established as an autonomous institution of UGC to assess and accredit HEIs in the country. The only mission with which NAAC was created that was just to stimulate the academic environment for the promotion of quality teaching and research in higher education. NAAC has been striving to provide leadership to HEIs in the country by boosting benchmarking as quality improvement tool in line with the international standards.

Over the past two decades, NAAC has been aiming to make quality the defining element of higher education in India through a combination of self and external quality evaluation, promotion and sustenance initiatives. However, the most pertinent question remains, "How far it has been able to achieve its vision and mission?" There has been no worthwhile study by anybody whatsoever to unravel this most pertinent question. However, there are clear indications that it has not been able to make any significant improvement in the quality of education offered by HEIs. It was expected that after putting HEIs to a comprehensive and rigorous assessment for accreditation, their academic pursuits will improve over a period of time, which will eventually help some of the institutions to figure at least in the list of world's top 200 or 300 universities. But as on today, none of the Indian universities figure in the list of top 200 or 300 universities. As per the QS World University Ranking-2021, none of the Indian universities/institutes could feature in the top 100, a total of eight institutes have found their place in the top 500, all these are IITs and IISc, Bangalore which does not come under the ambit of NAAC. Such a gloomy picture is a reflection of poor performance of our universities at the global stage, which eventually reflects the failure of this important regulatory body, i.e. NAAC.

More than 800 universities and colleges so far have been assessed and accredited by NAAC more than once or twice. Around 60% of these institutions have been granted A+ and above grade which means that these institutions are able to deliver quality education of a highest standard. This raises a question, then why none of these institutions are even able to make a place in the list of top 500 global institutions. This may be due to the fact that either NAAC's quality parameters are not in line with the global ranking agencies or the assessing teams have miserably failed to assess HEIs thoroughly and honestly. The fact of the matter is that earlier NAAC's assessment was only subjective peer reviewed, thus prone to human error and bias. To improve upon this and other shortcomings arising from the changing realities nationally and globally, NAAC launched its revised Assessment and Accreditation Framework in July 2017, which marks an explicit paradigm shift, making the whole process ICT enabled, objective, transparent, scalable and robust. It is also that while comparing the assessment parameters of NAAC with

Times-QS Rankings, there is a mismatch between their assessment parameters. This raises a Million Dollar Question that is does the meaning of the term 'Quality Education' differs for different ranking agencies which ordinarily should mean same thing for every agency, may be with minor variations to account for some perceptual differences?

The central focus of Education Policies, Accreditation Councils, HEIs and other related agencies is on quality teaching and research, but without precisely having a very clear perspective of the term 'Quality Education'. Unless and until the term quality is defined precisely and accurately, we are likely to end up heading towards a dead end. The key for all this lies in the fact that we need to know what 'Quality' in higher education is all about. The term 'Quality' in management refers to the ability of a manufacturer or service provider to provide on demand the products or services that customers find of great value, i.e. which meets or exceeds the expectations of the customers. This gives rise to two pertinent questions; One, 'Who are the Customers of HEIs'? Second, 'What are their expectations from HEIs operating in the Indian Landscape?' The customers of HEIs includes; students/parents, potential employers and the society in general. The students/parents want an educational opportunity that develops their overall personality so as to enable them to find a gainful employment with ease, while as potential employers require HEIs to provide human resources who are competent to manage socio-economic domains professionally and efficiently in their chosen fields of specialisation. The society wants HEIs to advance social and community development, foster economic competitiveness, and improve quality of life by innovating new technologies, processes and find plausible solutions to the socio-economic problems being faced at the local, national and global levels respectively. Therefore, to develop students for gainful employment, deliver capable and competent brains to employers, and diagnose socio-economic and other problems confronting the economies and the society with plausible solutions, the most critical elements of quality education includes Quality of Academic Programmes; Enabling Teaching-Learning Environment; Availability of Requisite Infrastructure and Learning Resources; Ecosystem for Quality Research; Effective

Leadership and Governance and Community Engagement and Social Services. NAAC uses almost the same parameters to assess the quality of education at higher education level. However, the key indicators used to assess the quality of some of these parameters need refinements.

Though from 2017, the accreditation process is claimed to have been made more robust, objective, transparent and scalable as well as ICT enabled, yet there are still some question marks, stemming from its data validation processes and integrity of the members of peer teams. It is known to one and all that the visiting peer teams though are being paid handsomely by NAAC, yet still they are found enjoying the five star hospitality of visiting institutions, thus posing a question mark on their credibility. Generally, vigour and resolve to undertake inspection thoroughly and objectively has largely been found missing among the assessors. It is in view of these and other limitations, NEP-2020 has recommended that onwards the assessment shall be arranged through independent 'Accrediting Institutions' supervised and overseen by NAAC. In US, the accreditation is a voluntary and non-governmental process in the sense that the whole process is carried out by the private accrediting agencies, duly recognised by the Department of Education. But ultimately this new process will yield due dividends only when credible and competent 'Accrediting Institutions' are involved and effectively monitored. Assigning assessment and accreditation process to nationally or internationally recognised 'Credit Rating' agencies like CARE, CRISIL, etc. would be a step in the right direction. Besides, the accreditation should be discipline/Dept. specific rather for an institution as a whole which is a universally accepted criterion. Some total of the scores of different Depts./Centres should become the overall institutional score. The Dept./Centre specific assessment will usher HEIs into greater competitiveness internally, thus will act as a force multiplier to continually achieve excellence in academic pursuits at each and every level.

NAAC, on the basis of Cumulative Grade Point Average (CGPA), assigns eight letter grades, viz., 'A++', 'A+', 'A', 'B++', 'B+', 'B', 'C', and 'D'. Institutions assigned letter grades from A++ to C are declared as accredited and the institutions which gets letter grade 'D' are declared as not accredited. The validity period of NAAC accreditation is five years, however, for third/ fourth cycle, it can be extended from five years to seven years, with a condition that they have obtained highest grade. This grading scale is too wide, as a result allows institutions to operate even with B+ or B or C grade, whose quality of education is low or very low, though ineligible for funding from Central Government. It is in view of this fact, we may need to revisit this grading scale on the pattern of US. In US, Accrediting Institutions use five point grading scale, viz., 'Outstanding' (3-4); 'Standard' (2.0-2.9); 'Acceptable' (2.0-2.8); 'Insufficient' (0-1.9) and Nule (less than 1.9). Institutions getting 'Outstanding Grade' needs no improvement and are required to get its rating reviewed after five years whereas 'Standard Grade' implies that such institutions may require to improve and are mandated to get its rating reviewed after 12 months. Institutions with 'Acceptable Grade' are granted temporary accredited status for one year. Such institutions must undergo a new accreditation within next 12 months and if full accreditation is not achieved by such institutions, the accreditation status is denied. Institutions getting 'Insufficient or Nule' grading are denied accreditation, however, can re-apply for accreditation after 12 months. The above system of grading implies that actually institutions with 'Outstanding' grade only are given full accreditation and the rest are either granted accreditation for one year or denied. This approach is more appropriate than the approach of NAAC because the accreditation process needs to be very strict and not based on a very loosely grading scale. The perception world over is that the US accreditation is a 'Gold Standard'.

As stated above, there are very serious question marks on peer team visits, therefore, there is an urgent need to relook at their current modus operandi used to assess and accredit institutions. To standardise the peer team visits, the following guidelines based on the best practices are recommended to achieve due results from the their visits:

- The peer team should consist of assessors belonging to all subjects/streams offered by the visiting HEI, however, each member shall be required to give an undertaking that he or she is or has not been in any way connected with the visiting HEI.

- Before visiting the HEI, the accrediting agency should organise a 'Pre-Visit Meeting' of the Peer Team Members to review the SSR with the purpose to decide about how to proceed to conduct the visit.
- Make an unscheduled visit to the institution and arrange all the logistics for the visit at their own.
- After having a meeting with the top administrators of HEI, subject specialists should visit to the departments and as per the SSR, check all the required documents, physical infrastructure, and have discussions with the faculty members, scholars, students and non-teaching staff in a very informal manner. Conduct Satisfaction Surveys wherever required.
- Assess and accredit Dept.-wise rather than the institution as a whole. Some total of the scores of different Depts./ Centres should become the overall institutional score. This will serve two purposes; One, accredit each department/ centre individually. Second, it will enable to differentiate between good and poor performers which in turn will cultivate a competitive culture within the institution.
- Exit meeting should be aimed only to thank the administration of the HEI rather than disclosing impressions about the institutions accreditation.
- Final Assessment Meeting of the members of the peer team should be conducted to decide about the revision of the computer-generated score on the basis of the verification of claims made in the SSR. Besides, a detailed report delineating the type of improvements that an institution shall have to make within a specified period of time shall have to be prepared for submission to NAAC.
- If the peer review team comes to the conclusion that the claims made in the SSR report were false and mere fabrications, the team shall be mandated to recommend panel action to be taken against the HEI to NAAC.

20

Assessment and Accreditation of Higher Education: Calls for Refinements of Key Indicators of Quality Parameters

Since 1994, NAAC has been involved in the assessment and accreditation of higher educational institutions in the country with a sole purpose to ensure that the quality educational pursuits are available to the learners by benchmarking and assessing quality of higher education. Based on the feedback received over a long period of time from various Consultative Meetings, Expert Group Meetings, and the academia during the Assessors Interaction Meetings, in 2017 NAAC launched the Revised Assessment and Accreditation Framework which is aimed to transform it from qualitative peer judgement to data-based quantitative evaluation having increased objectivity, transparency and ICT enabled. However, still there remains number of question marks particularly about the data validation processes and integrity of the members of peer teams. NEP-2020 has recommended that now onwards the assessment and accreditation will be done by the duly recognised Accrediting Agencies which hopefully will take care of the issues of the lack of integrity and vigour and enthusiasm of peer team members. The NAAC uses seven parameters to assess quality of education which to a large extent reflects the quality of teaching, research and extension activities but the key indicators used to assess the quality of each of these parameters needs some refinements so as to make them more meaningful which has been attempted as under:

Quality of Academic Programmes

The main stay of HEIs is to offer academic programmes leading to graduate and research degrees. Therefore, the success or failure of HEIs depends upon the quality of their academic programmes. The graduates of IIMs, IITs and some other leading HEIs are getting lucrative job offers from industries and other entities located all over the world as soon as they complete their degrees. They are in high demand because the quality of their academic programmes are perceived of very high quality. It would be really unrealistic to expect every institution to be of the same standard but at least the students of other HEIs also have the right to get such a quality education that enables them to get gainfully employed with ease. Given these hard facts, it is the duty of all HEIs and the regulators to ensure educational opportunities offered by HEIs should be of standard quality. As such, while assessing the HEIs for accreditation, one of the important indicators has to be the quality of academic programmes in the offing. The 'Quality of Academic Programmes' is mainly reflected in the indicators like demand for the academic programmes, and the quality of curricular. The demand for a course can be measured in terms of the Ratio of applicants per seat; Minimum cut-off for admissions, and Diversity of the applicants. The quality of curricular should be assessed in terms of the Process used to design and update the curricular; Autonomy to the faculty in designing course curriculum; Flexibility in terms of choice of non-credit courses; Freedom to choose from a basket of courses, to complete the degree at their own convenient pace, freedom to exit and re-enter; Career orientation and Provision of internships. All the more important will be to have an expert review of the course curriculum so as to assess whether it is updated and of a standard quality. More appropriate would be to see how it compares with the course curriculum of leading institutions. In terms of outcomes, the quality of academic programmes need to be measured in terms of the intended outcomes of the programme like, *campus placements, and through course objective survey.*

Enabling Teaching-Learning Environment

It refers to an ecosystem that facilitates effective and meaningful learning of the learners which consists of Quality of students; Adequacy of qualified and committed teachers; Merit-based career progression and management; Engaging and experiential teaching pedagogy; Quality, accountability and transparency in assessment; Co-curricular activities; and Student support and progression. The quality of students can be assessed in terms of competitiveness of admission process and minimum cut-off in admissions. The adequacy of qualified and committed faculty should be determined in terms of Minimum number of faculty members at different levels specified by the regulator for the academic programmes and the no. of sanctioned posts; Ratio of sanctioned positions filled to the total sanctioned positions; Ratio of permanent faculty to the contractual faculty; Ratio of faculty members with Ph.D./Post Doc. to the total faculty; and Ratio of faculty members teaching courses/related courses in which having Ph.D. To ensure each faculty member feels enthusiastic, engagėd, and motivated towards advancing his/her students, institution, and profession, among other things calls for having a merit-based career progression and management in place. The key indicators specifying this aspect of faculty should include; Ratio of faculty members promoted in time, workload of faculty members not excessive to be measured by dividing the total no. of courses by the total no. of faculty members; Teacher-student ratio, Percentage of faculty members who have attended FDPs, workshops and other developmental programmes; and Percentage of faculty members awarded prestigious fellowships. Faculty Satisfaction Survey with respect to quality of merit-based career progression and management is must.

The teaching pedagogy should be diagnostic, remedial and improvement oriented rather than reactive in nature, therefore, calls for a paradigm shift from summative semester-end examination system to a continuous and comprehensive formative system which can be measured in terms of the Percentage of marks earmarked for continuous assessment in the form of class tests, case studies, role playing, projects, presentations, and field surveys; Frequency with which feedback is shared with the students about their performance based on class test, etc.; How far teaching pedagogy and assessment used comply with the programme goals and learning outcomes of each course?; and the extent of ICT used in teaching. There is no denying the fact that offline and e-learning can complement each other. Therefore, to derive due dividends from modern teaching technologies, HEIs should facilitate to use "Flipped Classroom Technique" where students are provided notes and pre-recorded lectures in advance and have discussion/debate to clear doubts in the offline or online mode. This will be reflected in student satisfaction survey as well.

Accountability and transparency on the one hand is essential to boost the credibility of the assessment system and on the other hand makes it learner friendly. This can be assessed by the indicators like; Percentage of courses for which proctored online and open book examinations are held, Mechanisms put in place to ensure course outcome based question papers; Mechanism for allowing students to see their answer copies before the declaration of final results; Percentage of grade appeals; Mechanism for decentralised grade appeal system; Average time taken to declare the semester end examination results and to address grade appeals. However, in the interest of authenticity of data, the whole system of examination and assessment should be ICT enabled. Student satisfaction survey regarding the above aspects of assessment would be essential.

The wholesome development of a learner also depends on his or her exposure and experience to the developments happening in the world around them which signifies the importance of co-curricular activities. Besides, students need support of all types to help them financially, emotionally which in turn calls for adequate systems of student support and progression. One can assess these aspects of enabling learning environment by a varied nature of co-curricular activities supported and conducted by the HEI by making a critical review of the mechanisms put in place for Mentoring and counselling and Career counselling and placements; Mechanism for funding topic-centred clubs and activities organized by students; No. of student exchange programmes organised; Percentage of students offered scholarships; No. of co-curricular programmes in which students of the dept. participated at local level, national level, international level; No. of panel discussions held on new developments taking place locally, nationally and globally by the dept; No. of talks delivered by the practitioners/policy makers on current issues; and No. of extension lectures delivered by the subject experts. Student Satisfaction Survey of Student Support and Progression will be needed to conduct to get feedback from the real stakeholders, i.e. students.

To assess the outcomes of enabling learning environment, there is a need to conduct the survey of Evaluation of Teaching by the students, Peers Evaluation and Self-evaluation by the faculty. Graduating student survey should also be conducted to seek a comprehensive feedback from the graduating students about all the aspects of their respective academic programmes and other related aspects. However, the results should be aimed to seek improvements in teaching rather than to meet the requirements for assessment and accreditation. Besides, teaching outcomes should be assessed in terms of; Percentage of students who got jobs as per their speciality immediately after completing their degrees, within next six months, within one year of graduation; Percentage of students who got jobs in other fields immediately after completing their degrees, within next six months and within one year of graduation; Percentage of students who got jobs as per their speciality in the govt. sector, local, national and international private sector companies of repute; Percentage of students satisfied with jobs they got; Percentage of students who have qualified civil services examination, NET/SET, JRF, Other professional and competitive examinations; and Percentage of students who have started their own businesses or joined family business. These aspects can be assessed through Survey of Recently Graduated Students.

Ecosystem for Quality Research

Apart from teaching, universities are also aimed to conduct research to invent new technologies, processes and find solutions to the socio-economic issues with an aim to advance social and community development, foster economic competitiveness, and improve quality of life. Evidences from the world's best universities throughout the history has shown that the best teaching and learning processes at higher education level occur in environments where there is also a strong culture of research and knowledge creation. But merely conducting research serves little or no purpose, what matters the most, is the quality of research? Conducting cutting edge research in the areas of biotechnology, nanotechnology, artificial intelligence, etc. is important for the country like India, which is striving hard to get a place of prominence at the global stage.

Existence of an ecosystem which not only facilitates but also makes researchers accountable for the conduct of quality research is necessary to exist. The key elements of such an ecosystem includes: Institutional Research Policy and Research Council; Administrative flexibility and support system for research; Policy of mentoring of young teachers; Facility and funding for incubation and technology development; Centre for patenting and Partnering; and Policy for consultancy, extension and collaborative research. Besides, to create a competitive culture throughout an institution, policy to recognise excellence in research and teaching is necessary to exist. It is also that to make everyone to conduct quality research, benchmarking for research, faculty and department-wise is required to establish. The research policy should define the thrust areas for research discipline and subject-wise which should be the responsibility of 'Research Council' consisting of Faculty Deans, College Principals, Policy Makers, Top Govt. functionaries of relevant departments, Nominees of Chambers of Industry, Trade & Commerce, Practitioners, and Prominent scientists/researchers. The key indicators to assess administrative flexibility and support should include, creation of separate administrative set-up to manage all aspects of research, mechanism for incentivization of the conduct of quality research, flexibility in administrative procedures, and budgetary allocation towards promoting research culture. There is greater focus now on incubation at all levels in the country, as a result lot of funding is being made available to the universities which are considered ideal places for such activities. This crucial activity will be assessed in terms of Funding generated; Availability of seed capital to Star-Ups; Infrastructure available for incubation and technology development; No. of start-ups successfully launched by the students; and No. of patents registered and no. of patents commercialized. The universities have also a role to outreach society, etc. to educate, aware and train people, which will be assessed by the Quantum of collaborative research done; Extent to which consultancy services offered; No. of working groups formed by the Govt., policy institutions, industry associations/federations in which faculty members acted as members; and No. of educational, awareness, and training programmes conducted. The key indicators for assessing that whether the excellence in research and teaching is being duly recognised by the institution should include: Policy for best teacher award, best researcher award, and policy for fast pacing of promotions in recognition of excellence in research and teaching; No. of faculty members awarded and promoted in recognition of excellence in teaching and research.

The outcomes based on research, innovations and extension, should be measured both in terms of 'Bibliometrics and Altmetrics' for each Dept. and the university as whole. While using bibliometrics, No. of books published; No. of research papers published in impact factor journals, indexed journals and other journals; No. of ongoing research projects; No. of research projects completed; Total funding mobalised for sponsored research from funding agencies; Citation Index, h index, and impact factor. In terms of Altmetrics; No. of patents filed and registered; No. of registered patents commercialised; No. of technological breakthroughs achieved; No. of citations of the research in public policy documents; No. of research models developed becoming part of industry practices; Frequency of discussions on research blogs about the research done in the university; Mainstream media coverage of the research done at the local, national and international level; and Bookmarks or reference managers. Collaborative Research done department-wise with the Govt. Depts., private sector, research centres and NGOs should be used to assess collaborative research. Similarly to assess the extent to which the university has provided a platform for debate and discussion or the participation of faculty in various discussion platforms, the key indicators should include; No. of conferences, seminars, workshops organised by the university; No. of times faculty members delivered key note addresses in the local, national and international conferences; No. of times faculty members acted as chairpersons/co-chairpersons of a technical session in the conferences organised at local, national and international level; No. of conferences/seminars organised at local, national and international level where faculty members presented papers; and No. of best paper or best presentation awards won by the faculty members in conferences/seminars organised at local, national and international level.

Infrastructure and Learning Resources

Achieving the goals of excellence in teaching and research to a great extent depends upon the adequacy and quality of infrastructure available to the faculty, supporting staff, scholars, and students. To assess the adequacy and quality of physical infrastructure, the key indicators includes: Pleasant classroom spaces fitted with modern teaching technology; Smart classrooms; Excess to high speed internet facility; Wi-Fi Campus; State-of-the-art labs; Libraries with rich collection of books, manuscripts, reports and research journals accessible both offline and online and access to all sorts of statistical data; Facilities of safe clean drinking water, clean working toilets, offices, and teaching supplies. It is the responsibility of an institution to ensure hostel accommodation to students and scholars coming from far-off places with living conditions which are affordable, comfortable, ensures privacy and offers an environment conducive to an academic pursuit and personal growth. Round the clock medical facilities are also necessary to exist to take care of medical emergencies of the campus residents and non-resident students and employees. The extracurricular activities are equally important to groom the overall personality of students. Therefore, the existence of all sorts of facilities for sports and other extracurricular activities are must like: Coaches; Infrastructural facilities for indoor and outdoor games, viz., playing fields, athletic tracks, all weather swimming pool, tennis courts, boats, etc. for adventure and water sports, tents, etc. for trekking and rock climbing; Halls for indoor games like, badminton, table tennis, gymnasium, billiards, weight lifting and above all modern health clubs with adequate gym facilities. Equally important is to provide students with adequate opportunities to participate in debates, competitions for art and paintings, cultural activities, music, literary activities, etc. both within and outside the university.

Specially abled students and employees require special attention so as to make their stay in the campus easy and hassle free which would require to put in place such an infrastructure in every nook and corner of the campus that will take care of their disabilities like: Provision of ramps in all buildings; Specially designed washrooms; Availability of hearing aids; Availability of transport facility exclusively meant for specially abled persons within the campus; Annual budgetary allocations for providing gadgets, etc. to the poor specially abled students; and concession in admission fee.

The quality and adequacy of physical infrastructure mainly can be assessed by the visiting peer team to the campuses. However, the outcome of some of the indicators can be assessed through documentary evidence for teaching technology in terms of; Percentage of classes fitted with modern teaching technology; Percentage of faculty members provided with dedicated desktops with printers and high-speed internet facility; Student-computer ratio, number of books, manuscripts, committee reports, statistical reports available in the library. The outcomes with respect to hostel accommodation should include: Percentage of total male and female applicants provided hostel accommodation; Percentage of male and female research scholar applicants provided hostel accommodation. The key indicators to assess the quality of medical facility should includes: No. of medical doctors available, type of medical facilities available; No. of ambulances available; and annual budgetary allocation for medicines, etc. With respect to extracurricular activities, the outcome indicators may include: No. of tournaments game-wise organised by HEI for male and female students; No. of teams participated; No. of inter university tournaments, game-wise organised by HEI for male and female students; and No. of teams participated; No. of tournaments won; No. of university students selected to represent the state and the country; No. of coaching camps organised in association with nationally acclaimed sportspersons; No. of quizzes, debates, cultural events, music or painting competitions organised at the state level, inter university level and number of prizes, medals won by HEI. To assess the level of satisfaction the surveys like: Satisfaction survey of hostellers; Satisfaction Survey of Students about infrastructural facilities available in the depts.; Satisfaction survey of faculty members; Satisfaction Survey of Students and scholars; Satisfaction survey of Employees; Satisfaction survey of participating students in different tournaments; and Satisfaction survey of participating students in debates, quizzes, competitions, etc. will be necessary to conduct.

Effective Leadership and Governance

The pivot around which rotates the entire edifice of teaching, research and extension is the leadership and governance with which a HEI is endowed. Among other things, leadership would need to have a very clear and realistic vision i.e. description of what an university would like to achieve in future and also requires to demonstrate energy and total commitment to the vision and mission continuously and visibly. Based on the vision, establishment of a long-term 'Institutional Strategic Plan' would be essential, the duration of which would depend upon the constraints of visibility and milestones to be accomplished. A "Strategic Planning Committee" will need to be constituted for framing a 'Strategic Plan', which sets the milestones to be achieved. While framing a 'Strategic Plan', the strategic committee is required to use "Top-down and Bottom-up Approach" which calls for prioritisation of strategic processes and programmes at all levels in the university. However, the implementation of a 'Strategic Plan' calls for having a robust Institutional Effectiveness Mechanism in place which is a whole process of aligning departmental vision and mission statements with that of an institution; in line with the goals, set performance targets for each faculty member, department/centre, faculty, and student support centres; measure actual performances and compare the same with the standard performances to find out variations if any and propose corrective actions to be taken to plug the gaps in targeted performances.

To make Institutional Effectiveness Mechanism to work effectively, the governance of human, financial and other material resources need to be managed professionally and effectively. To manage human resources effective, the need for having a robust Human Resource Management systems in place to professionally manage manpower planning, timely recruitment, performance appraisal, transfer policy, promotions and training and development of human resources in an efficient manner. Even to ensure quality human resources for achieving academic excellence, among other things the management of HEI would need to manage its financial resources efficiently so that there is no constraint of financial resources. This in turn calls for putting in place an efficient financial management system which aims to mobilise requisite funds both internally and externally and ensure efficient utilisation of financial resources to yield maximum dividends. Conversely, if the system is not efficient, the organisation is bound to suffer from the lack of financial resources or mismanagement of financial resources. The research has revealed that the organisations which are heavily dependent on others, their managements are generally overburden with financial problems thus 'Becomes Myopic'.

Culture of participative decision-making and autonomy is equally important to foster spirit for teamwork which allows to achieve organizational goals as it ensures unity in the workplace, offers differing perspectives and feedback, offers greater learning opportunities and promotes workplace synergy. Therefore, the management systems should value and respect all campus constituents, celebrate diversity, and embrace shared governance by fostering inclusiveness in decision-making. E-governance practices are highly important to achieve greater degree of efficiency in governance. The transparency and accountability act as a founding pillar for effective governance.

The key indicators of leadership are reflected in its long-term strategic plan, and a system of institutional effectiveness. The robustness of human resource management systems will be assessed by analysing the Policies for recruitment and appointments; Performance appraisal system; Policies for promotions, trainings and development; and Employee grievance redressal mechanism. The key indicators to assess quality of HRM practices includes: Ratio of non-teach staff to teaching staff; Ratio of technical staff to the total staff; Ratio of computer literate staff to the total staff; Percentage of staff positions vacant to the total available sanctioned positions at different levels; and Percentage of employee grievances to the total employees. The efficiency of the management of financial resources will be assessed in terms of the systems of accounting information and budgeting; Frequency of reporting financial statements; Percentage of own revenue sources to the total revenues; Percentage of academic expenses to total revenue expenses; Ratio of plan to non-plan expenditures; Percentage of scholarship and fellowship expenses to total non-plan expenses; Percentage of co-curricular and extracurricular expenses to total revenue expenses; Percentage of conferences, seminars, debate and workshop expenses to total revenue expenses; Percentage of faculty development expenses to total non-plan expenses; and Percentage of books and journal expenses to total expenses. The key indicators of e-governance will consist of: Extent to which receipt and payment system is online; Extent of filling of online admission, examination and other forms by the students; Extent of online declaration of examination results; and Online student grievance redressal system. The indicators to assess the accountability and transparency of the governance system will include, internal audit, annual financial audit, stock audit, book audit, and cost and works audit and the extent to which different stakeholders namely, faculty members, non-teaching staff, students, scholars, nominees of different employee bodies/associations and alumni allowed to participate in decision-making. To allow easy access to the information pertaining to different aspects of governance, the administration shall be required to circulate all policy documents among all the concerned, viz., Recruitment and promotion policies/rules; Service Rules, Accounting policy, Audit reports, Library policy, Admission policy, Grade appeal policy, Hostel accommodation and residence policy, Policy for Anti Plagiarism, Fire Safety Policy and Policy for sexual harassment redressal.

Social Responsibility and Distinctiveness

Apart from the core responsibility of offering opportunities for quality teaching and research, as being the highest seats of learning, HEIs have responsibility towards the greater good of the society at large. Towards this goal, universities have responsibility in the areas of community engagement and service, environmental education, and value-based education. It has also a responsibility to ensure equity and access to education particularly to the students belonging SEDGs. Towards environmental education there should a conscious attempt on the part of HEIs to educate and aware the students and the society at large about the issues like; climate change, pollution, waste management, sanitation, forest and wildlife conservation and energy conservation. Within the campus, HEIs are required to take measures for rainwater harvesting, waste recycling, carbon neutral and green practices. The curricular should also lay focus on value-based education by aiming to build character so as to enable learners to be ethical. The key indicators of equity and access to the weaker sections of the society includes: Providing financial assistance and scholarships to socio-economically disadvantaged students; Make admissions processes more inclusive, develop bridge courses for students that come from disadvantaged educational backgrounds and provide socio-emotional and academic support and mentoring for all such students through suitable counselling and mentoring programmes.

Final Word

Apart from making refinements to the various key indicators of quality as suggested above, NAAC needs to change modus operandi of conducting the assessment for accreditation completely. There are question marks about how come Members of Peer Visit Team can enjoy the hospitality of the visiting institutions. How come they seek inputs from different stakeholders who have been selected by the management of visiting institution rather doing at their own randomly? Verifiability of data submitted through SSR for its authenticity is difficult given the current framework which is more subjective in nature. In the current framework, there is a mention of third-party validation of data. Given the modus operandi in vogue, the third-party validation is difficult and whatever little scope it offers, that is subject to manipulations. It is perhaps these and other limitations of existing framework/process which made the architects of NEP-2020 to recommend assessment and accreditation to be done by the independent rating agencies. However, to derive the due dividends form this useful exercise, the framework for assessment need total revamping to align with the world's best practices.

Quality Parameters

Quality Parameter 1: Quality of Academic Programmes (150)

P1	Indicators	Minimum/ Maximum Benchmark	Maxi. Score	Validation Process
P1.1a	**Demand for Academic Programmes**		**(10)**	
	• Ratio of applicants per seat.	>30 : 1 20 : 1 <10 : 1	05 04 03	Admission Records available on the website
	• Minimum cut-off for admissions	> 70% 60% - 70% < 70%	05 04 03	
P1.1b	**Diversity of the Applicants**		**(10)**	
	• %age of Students belonging to the immediate Geographical area	<60%	04	Admission Records
	• %age of students belonging to the other parts of the state	>20%	02	
	• %age of students belonging to the other states	>20% >10%	03 02	
	• %age of students belonging to the other countries			

P1.1c	**Quality of Curricular** (A) Process used to design and update the curricular: • Constitution of BOS: (i) All faculty members (ii) Subject Experts (iii) Nominee of School Education Dept. (iv) Practitioners from reputed company/ organisation (v) Alumni Representatives.	 Yes 3 2 (Subject Experts) 2 (Qualified Professionals) 3 (Prominent Alumni)	**(32)** 03	 Copy of University Statutes & Approved BOS of all Departments
	(B) Frequency with which BOS Meeting is Convened.	< 3 Years > 5 Years	03 02	Minutes of BOS meetings
	(C) The Intended outcomes of each academic Programme offered by the university are clearly delineated in the Curricular which truly reflects the essence of the programme and are realistic and achievable.	* Yes	05	Expert Committee Review Report
	(D) The course structure of each academic programme is designed in a manner that is in consistent with the Programmes intended outcomes along with the teaching pedagogy and method of assessment to be used to achieve the intended outcomes of the course.	** Yes	05	Expert Committee Review Report

	(E) Autonomy to the faculty in designing course Curriculum	***Complete	**05**	Expert Committee Review Report & Variations in Teaching pedagogy & Assessment
	(F) Percentage of syllabus revision carried out during the last 5 years in each academic programme offered by the university	>35% 25% - 35%	05 04	Expert Committee Review Report
	(G) Percentage of new courses introduced to the total number of courses across all programs offered during the last five years	>15% 10% - 15%	06 04	Expert Committee Review Report
P1.1d	**Flexibility in Terms of Choice**		**(20)**	
	• Non-credit courses.	One course in each semester	02	University Statutes & Expert Committee Review Report & Student Satisfaction Survey
	• Freedom to choose from a basket of courses.	CBCS Choice to choose courses within a maxi Limit	06	
	• Freedom to complete the degree at their own convenient pace.		05	
	• Freedom to exit and re-enter.	Yes	04	
	• Shelf Life of Credits already earned.	2 Years	03	

P1.1e	**Employability of the Programme** • Average percentage of programmes offered by the University having focus on: (i) Employability. (ii) Entrepreneurship. (iii) Skill Development. • Percentage of students who have undertaken: (i) Field Surveys/Visits. (ii) Research Projects. (iii) Internships. • Type of companies with whom the university has MOU for Internship and associateship of Students: (i) Companies of national repute (ii) Companies of local repute (iii) Other companies	100% professional and Technical courses 60% - 80% of courses 30% - 50% of courses 30% - 50% 30% - 50% All professional and Technical courses 50% - 75% 25% - 50% 0.0% - 25%	**(33)** 05 01-03 01-03 02-04 02-04 05 02-05 01-03 0-01	Expert Committee Review Report Official Records MOUs
P1.1f	**Course Objective Survey** • Avg. Percentage of academic programmes for which course objective survey conducted during the last 5 years. • Percentage of courses for which course objective survey undertaken & where revisions were made based on the feedback of surveys during the last 5 years	65% - 95% 45% - 75%	**(10)** 02-05 02-05	Official Records & disclosure on the Official Website of the university Expert Committee Review Report

P1.1g	**Campus Placement**		**(25)**	
	• Avg. Percentage of students of Professional courses who got placed in nationally reputed companies per year.	<10%	01	Official Records & disclosure on the Official Website of the university
		>10% - 30%	02-03	
		>30% - 50%	04-06	
		>50% - 80%	07-10	
	• Percentage of students of Non-Professional courses who got placed in Nationally reputed companies or Govt./Semi Govt. Depts.	>05% - 10%	01-02	
		>10% - 15%	03-04	
		>15%	05	
P1.1h	**Expert Review of the Course Curriculum**		**(10)**	
	(To be done by the Accrediting Agency through subject experts by comparing with the curriculum of Leading Institutions)	90% - 95% parity	10	Expert Committee Review Report
		<90% - 80%	08	
		<80% - 70%	07	
		<70% - 60%	06	
		<60% - 50%	05	
		<50%	Zero	

Quality Parameter 2: Enabling Teaching-Learning Environment (300)

P2	Indicators	Minimum Benchmark	Maxi. Score	Validation
P2.1a	**Quality of Students**		**(15)**	
	• Competitiveness of Admission Process: Admissions done on the basis of Admission test at the:			
	(i) National Level	10% - 15% Courses	2-3	
	(ii) State Level	25% - 50% Courses	2-4	
	(iii) Local Level	50% - 75% Courses	1-2	Admission Records
	(iv) Graduation Merit	0.0% - 10% Courses	0-1	
	• Minimum cut-off in admissions:			
	(i) Professional & Technical Courses	80% - 90%	1-2	
	(ii) PG Courses & Integrated Courses	50% - 70% 40% - 50%	1-2	
	(iii) UG Courses		0-1	

P2.1b	Adequacy of Qualified and Committed Faculty		(50)	
	• Ratio of sanctioned posts to the Minimum number of faculty positions specified by the regulator for each programme.	>90% 71% - 90% 30% - 70%	10 8-9 3-7	
	• Ratio of positions filled to the total sanctioned positions.	>90% 71% - 90% 30% - 70%	10 8-9 3-7	Official Records
	• Ratio of permanent faculty to the contractual faculty.	>90% 71% - 90%	10 8-9	
	• Ratio of faculty members with Ph.D./Post Doc. to the total faculty.	30% - 70% >90% 71% - 90%	3-7 10 8-9	
	• Ratio of faculty members teaching courses/related courses in which having Ph.D.	30% - 70% >90% 71% - 90% 30% - 70%	3-7 10 8-9 3-7	
P2.1c	**Merit-Based Career Progression and Management**		**(55)**	
	• Average percentage of faculty members promoted within:			
	(i) Three months from the due date.	>90% 71% - 90% 60% - 70% <60%	10 8-9 6-7 5	Official Records
	(ii) Four months from the due date.	>90% 71% - 90% 60% - 70% <60%	 8 6-7 4-5	
	(iii) Six Months from the due date.	>90% 71% - 90% 60% - 70% <60%	3 7 5-6 4-3	
	• Percentage of faculty members whose Workload has been as per UGC n0orm or less than that.	>90% 71% - 90% 60% - 70% <60% 1:05 - 1 :10 1:11 - 1:15 >1:15	2 6 5-4 3-2 1 5-4 3-2	Time Table
	• Teacher-student ratio:	1:05 - 1 :15	1	
	(i) Professional & Technical Courses	1:15 - 1:25 >1:25	5-4 3-2	Admission Records
	(ii) PG & Integrated Courses	1:10 - 1 :20 1:20 - 1:30	1 5-4	
	(iii) UG Courses	>1:30	3-2 1	Admission Records

	• Percentage of faculty members who have attended FDPs, workshops and other developmental programmes per year.	41% - 50% 31% - 40% 20% - 30%	4-5 2-3 1-2	
	• Average percentage of full time teachers who have received awards, recognition, fellowships from Government/Govt. recognised bodies/Industry during the last five years at the State, National, and International Level.	10% - 15% 10% - 05% 0.0% - 05%	4-5 2-3 1-2	Official Records
P2. 1d	**Engaging and Experiential Teaching Pedagogy**		(30)	
	• Average Percentage of courses where Continuous & Comprehensive Formative System is in operation.	> 90% 80% - 90% 70% - 80%	5 3-4 2-3	Expert Committee Review
	• Average Percentage of marks for continuous assessment in the form of Class Tests, Case Studies, Role Playing, Projects, Presentations, & Field Surveys.	>50% 30% - 40% 20% - 30%	5 3-4 2-3	Student Survey & Review of Curricular
	• Frequency with which feedback is shared with the students about their performance based on class test, etc.	3 Weeks Monthly Midterm	5 4 3	Student Survey & Review of Curricular
	• Average Percentage of courses where teaching pedagogy & assessment used comply with the programme goals and learning outcomes.	> 90% 80% - 90% 70% - 80%	5 3-4 2-3	Student Survey & Review of Curricular Physical Verification

	• Average Percentage of courses where modern teaching technology is used in teaching-learning process. • Average Percentage of courses where both offline and e-learning methods are used to complement each other through a "Flipped Classroom Technique"	> 90% 80% - 90% 70% - 80% > 25% 15% - 25% 5% - 15%	5 3-4 2-3 5 3-4 2-3	Student Survey & Review of Curricular
P2. 1e	**Quality, Accountability and Transparency in Assessment**		(32)	
	• Average percentage of courses for which proctored online and open book examinations held.	> 25% 10% - 20% < 10%	5 3-4 2	Student Survey & Review of Curricular
	• Average percentage of programmes and courses where question papers used are in line with intended course outcomes.	> 90% 80% - 90% 70% - 80%	5 3-4 2-3	Student Survey & Review of QPs
	• Policy for 'Right of the Students' to see their answer copies before the declaration of results & for decentralised grade appeal system.	Yes*	1	Written Policy
	• Average percentage of programmes/courses, students of which are allowed to see their answer copies before the declaration of final results.	> 90% 80% - 90% 70% - 80%	5 3-4 1-2	Student Survey
	• Average Percentage of grade appeals for all the courses every year.	<5% 10% - 20% 20% - 30%	5 4-3 3-2	Official Records
	• Average percentage of courses where the semester-end examination results are declared within a period of from the Date of Examination	<2 Weeks 2-3 weeks >3 weeks	5 4-3 2	Official Records & Student Survey

	• Average time taken to address grade appeals. • Based on the continuous and comprehensive assessment, remedial steps taken to improve the learning of slow learners, like class tests, Assignments, Counselling are used.	< 1 Week 1-2 weeks 2 weeks & above Yes*	5 4-3 2 1	Official Records & Student Survey Student Survey
P2. 1f	**Student Progression and Support** • Mechanism for Mentoring and Counselling. • Ratio of students to mentor for academic and other related issues. • Mechanisms for career counselling and placements. • Average percentage of students benefited by career counselling and guidance for competitive examinations offered by the Institution every year. • Mechanism for funding topic-centred clubs and activities organized by students. • No. of activities of student clubs funded each year per academic programme. • Total amount provided for funding topic-centred clubs and activities organized by students each year Dept.-wise. • No. of student exchange programmes organised per year.	 Yes <1:20 1:20 - 1:30 1:30 - 1:50 Yes >50% 25% - 50% 10% - 25% Yes >10 8-9 6-7 > ₹ 70,000 60,000 - 69,000 50,000 - 59,000 >10 8-9 Less than 7	**(100)** 1 5 4-3 2-1 1 5 3-4 1-2 1 5 3-4 1-2 5 3-4 1-2 5 3-4 1-2	 Written Policy Official Records Student Survey Written Policy Official Records Budgetary Allocations & Official Records Official Records

	• Average percentage of students benefited from scholarships and concessions in fee provided by the institution, Government and non-government agencies (NGOs) every year (other than the students receiving scholarships under the government schemes for reserved categories).	>15% 10% - 15% 05% - 9%	5 3-4 1-2	Official Records
	• No. of co-curricular programmes in which students participated each year dept.-wise at: Local level, National level, and International level.	> 5 3-4 2-1	5 3-4 1-2	Official Records
	• No. of panel discussions held by each dept. on new developments taking place each year: Locally, Nationally, and Globally.	> 5 3-4 1-2	5 3-4 1-2	Official Records
	• No. of talks delivered by the practitioners/policy makers on current issues in each dept. each year.	> 5 3-4 1-2	5 3-4 1-2	Official Records
	• No. of extension lectures delivered by the nationally reputed subject experts/ practitioners in each dept. each year.	> 5 3-4 1-2	5 3-4 1-2	Official Records
	• Average percentage of students qualifying in state/national/international level examinations during the last five years (e.g., NET/SLET/GATE/GMAT/ CAT/GRE/TOEFL/Civil Services/State government examinations)	>20% 15% - 20% 10% - 14%	5 3-4 1-2	Official Records

	• Percentage of recently graduated students who have progressed to higher education (previous graduating batch): (i) UG to PG (ii) PG to PhD (iii) PhD to Post-doctoral	>50% 40% - 50% 30% - 40% >20% 15% - 20% 05% - 14% >2% 1% - 2% <0.99%	3 2 1 3 2 1 3 2 1	Admission Records
	• Alumni Association/ Chapters registered with a written constitution and elected body. • Number of Meetings held every year. • Alumni contribution during the last five years (INR in lakhs)	Yes Twice >75 50 - 75 25 - 49	1 2 5 3-4 1-2	Written Constitution Minutes of Meetings Bank Account Details
P2. 1g	**Outcomes of Enabling Learning Environment** • E-content is developed by teachers: (i) For e-PG-Pathshala (ii) For CEC (Undergraduate) (iii) For SWAYAM (iv) For other MOOCs platform (v) For NPTEL/NMEICT/ any other Government Initiatives (vi) For Institutional LMS	 25% 50% 75% 5%	**30**	

Quality Parameter 3: Ecosystem for Quality Research (250)

P3	Indicators	Minimum/ Maximum Benchmark	Maxi. Score	Validation
P3. 1a	**Institutional Research Policy and Research Council**		**(10)**	
	• Has a Research Policy which among other things identify thrust areas for research discipline and subject-wise.	*Yes	1	Expert Review of Policy Document
	• Has Constituted very inclusive Research Council with representation from industry, NGOs, Govt. and others.	*Yes	1	Expert Review of Constitution of the Council
	• Frequency with which Research Council met.	Once a Year		Minutes of the meetings
	• Frequency with which Research Council has Reviewed Research Conducted so far.	After Every 3 Years	1	Review Report of the council
	• Review Report of the Research Council about the Quality of Research Conducted so far.	Quite Satisfactory Satisfactory Unsatisfactory	1 5 4 0	Review Report of the council
	• Has well-drafted Code of Ethics for research and the institution ensures its implementation in letter and spirit.	*Yes	1	Expert Review of Code of Ethics

P3. 1b	**Administrative Flexibility and Support System for Research**		**(35)**	
	• Has Created separate administrative set-up to manage all aspects of research.	*Yes	1	Expert Review of Administrative. Structure
	• Has mechanism for incentivization of the conduct of quality research.	*Yes	1	Expert Review of Incentivisation policy
	• Budgetary allocation towards promoting research culture.	>1% of Revenue Budget	4	Budget Copy
		<0.5-1% of Revenue Budget	3	
	• Number of workshops/ seminars conducted during the last five years on:			
	(i) Research methodology.	>150	5	
		100 - 150	3-4	Official Records
		<100	1-2	
	(ii) Intellectual Property Rights (IPR).	>20	5	Official Records
		10 - 20	3-4	
		<20	2	Official Records
	(iii) Entrepreneurship skill development.	>100	5	
		50 - 100	3-4	
		<50	2	Official Records
	• The institution provides seed money to its teachers for research (average per year INR in Lakhs)	>50		
		25 - 50	5	
		<25	3-4	
			2	
	• Institution has the following facilities to support research:			
	(i) Central Instrumentation Centre	*Yes	1	
	(ii) Animal House/Green House		1	Physical Verification
	(iii) Museum		1	
	(iv) Media laboratory/		1	
	Studios		1	
	(v) Business Lab			
	(vi) Research/Statistical		1	
	Databases		1	
	(vii) Moot court		1	
	(viii) Theatre		1	
	(ix) Art Gallery			

P3. 1c	**Policy of Mentoring Young Teachers**		**(20)**	
	• Has the Policy for Mentoring of Young Teacher	*Yes	1	Expert Review of the Policy
	• Average percentage of Young Teachers Mentored per year.	>70% 50% - 70%	6 4-5	Official Records
	• List of Prominent Academicians with whom Mentoring agreement signed.	>50% Yes	3 1	Official Records
	• Expenditure Incurred on Mentoring per year (₹ in Lakhs).	>15 10 -15 <10	6 4-5 3	Official Records
	• Satisfaction Survey of Young Teachers who have been mentored to assess their satisfaction level.	> 90% 60% - 90 % >60%	6 4-5 3	Survey Records
P3. 1d	**Facility and Funding for Incubation and Technology Development**		**(40)**	
	• Has incubation and technology development Centre with state of the art Infrastructure and Management.	Yes	2	Physical Verification and Review of Management set-up
	• Funds generated for incubation per year (₹ in Crores).	>15 10 - 15 <10	6 4-5 3	Official Records
	• Average amount of seed capital provided to Start-Ups per year (₹ in Crores).	>5 3 - 5 <3	6 4-5 3	Official Records
	• No. of start-ups successfully launched by the students per year.	>5 3 - 5 <3	10 8-9 5	Documentary Evidence
	• No. of patents registered per year.	>15 10 - 15 <10	6 4-5 3	Documentary Evidence
	• No. of registered patents commercialized every year.	>5 3 - 5 <3	10 8-9 5	Documentary Evidence

P3. 1e	**Extension & Collaborative Research**		**(20)**	
	• Institution has a policy on consultancy including revenue sharing between the institution and the individual researchers and encourages its faculty to undertake consultancy.	*Yes	1	Expert Review of Policy Document
	• Revenue generated from consultancy and corporate trainings during the last five years (INR in Lakhs).	>50 40 - 50 <40	6 4-5 3	Official Records
	• Quantum of collaborative research done with other institutions/research establishments/industry for research.	>2.5% of the total sponsored research done 2.5% - 1.5% of the total sponsored research done <1.5% of the total sponsored research done	5 4-3 2	Expert Review of the Evidence
	• No. of faculty members who have worked as one of the members of the working groups formed by the Govt., policy institutions, industry associations/federations for policy formulation, etc.	>0.5% of faculty members <0.5% of faculty members	3 2	Official Records
	• No. of educational, awareness, and training programmes conducted on the issues concerning the economy and society every year.	>50 30 - 50 <30	5 3-4 2	Official Records

P3. 1f	**Policy for the Recognition of Excellence in Research and Teaching** • Has a Policy for recognition of excellence in teaching and research?	 *Yes	**(10)** 2	Expert Review of the Policy Document
	• No. of faculty members promoted in recognition of excellence in research and teaching.	>10% 5% - 10% >.5%	6 4-5 3	Official Records
	• Frequency of awarding excellence in research and teaching: (i) Best teacher award (ii) Best Young Teacher Award (iii) Best researcher award (iv) Best Young Researcher Award	 Yearly basis Yearly basis 3 Year basis 3 Year basis	2	Official Record
P3. 1g	**Outcomes Based on Research, Innovations and Extension-Dept.-wise** • Percentage of departments with UGC-SAP, CAS, DST-FIST, DBT, ICSSR and other recognitions by national and international agencies (Data for the latest completed academic year	 >30% 20% - 30% < 20%	**90** 5 3-4 2	Official Records
	• Extramural funding for Research (Grants sponsored by the non-government sources such as industry, corporate houses, international bodies for research projects) endowments, Chairs in the University during the last five years (INR in Crores)	>15 10 - 15 <10	10 8-9 7	Official Records

	• Grants for research projects sponsored by the government agencies during the last five years (INR in Crores)	>30 20 - 30 <20	6 4-5 3	Official Records
	• Number of research projects per teacher funded by government and non-government agencies during the last five years	<3 2-3 <2	3 2 1	Documentary Evidence
	• Number of awards/ recognitions received for research/innovations by the institution/teachers/research scholars/students during the last five years	>200 100 - 150 <100	5 3-4 2	Official Record
	• Number of Ph.D.'s awarded per approved research guide during the last five years.	More than 5 3-4 <03	5 3-4 2	Admission Records
	• Number of JRFs, SRFs, Post Doctoral Fellows, Research Associates and other research fellows enrolled in the institution during the last five years	>750 500 - 750 <500	5 3-4 2	Documentary Evidence
	• Percentage of teachers receiving national/international fellowships/financial support from various agencies for advanced studies/research during the last five years	>15% 10% - 15% <10%	5 3-4 2	Documentary Evidence
	Research Outcomes in terms of Bibliometrics			
	• No. of books published by the faculty members during the last 5 years.	>175 150 - 175 <150	5 3-4 2	Documentary Evidence
	• No. of research papers published per teacher per year in:			
	(i) Impact Factor Journals/ Indexed Journals	>4 2 - 3 1	9 7-8 5	Documentary Evidence
	(ii) Other Journals.	>2 1 - 2 1	4 2-3 1	

	• No. of ongoing research projects per teacher per year.	>01	5	Documentary Evidence
	• No. of research projects completed per teacher per year.	<01	5	Documentary Evidence
	• Average Percentage of citations, etc. per teacher at the end of the 5th year:			
	(i) Citation index,	>200 150 - 200 <150	5 3-4 2	Documentary Evidence
	(ii) h index.	>100 75 - 100 <75	5 3-4 2	
	(iii) cumulative Impact factor.	>200 150 - 200 <150	5 3-4 2	Documentary Evidence
P3. 1h	**Opportunity for Debate and Discussion or Participation of Faculty in Various Discussion Forums**		**(25)**	
	• No. of conferences, seminars, workshops organised by the university year-wise.	>1 per Dept. 0.5 per Dept.	5 4	Documentary Evidence
	• Percentage of faculty members who have delivered keynote addresses every year in the conferences organised at: Local level National level International level	>20% of Professors 10% - 20% of Professors <10%	5 3-4 2	Documentary Evidence
	• Percentage of faculty members who acted as chairpersons/ co-chairpersons of a technical session in the conferences organised at: Local level National level International level	>30% of Professors 20% - 30% of Professors <20%	5 3-4 2	Documentary Evidence

	• Percentage of faculty members who have attended conferences/seminars and presented papers, organised at: Local level National level International level	>50% of Professors 40% - 50% of Professors <40%	5 3-4 2	Documentary Evidence
	• Percentage of faculty members who have been awarded best paper or best presentation awards in the conferences/seminars organised at: Local level National level International level	>10% of Professors 05% - 10% of Professors <05%	5 3-4 2	Documentary Evidence

Quality Parameter-4: Infrastructure and Learning Resources (150)

P4	Indicators	Minimum/ Maximum Benchmark	Maxi. Score	Validation
P4.1a	**Adequacy and Quality of Physical Infrastructure**		**(34)**	
	• Percentage of pleasant classroom spaces fitted with modern teaching technology.	>90% 80% - 90% < 80%	4 2-3 1	Physical Verification and Student Satisfaction Survey
	• Percentage no. of Smart classrooms Dept.-wise.	>25% 20% - 25% <25%	4 2-3 1	Physical Verification
	• Excess to high-speed internet facility and Wi-Fi Campus.	Yes	3	Documentary Evidence & Student Satisfaction Survey
	• Percentage of Science Depts. having required Labs with State of the art facilities.	>90% 80% - 90% <80%	4 2-3 1	Documentary Evidence & Student Satisfaction Survey
	• Student-computer ratio where IT is a part of the syllabus.	1: 1 1:2	3 2	Documentary Evidence & Student Satisfaction Survey

	• Libraries with rich collection of books, manuscripts, reports and research journals accessible both offline and online and access to all sorts of statistical data bases.	To the best satisfaction of all students and scholars	3	Documentary Evidence & Student Satisfaction Survey
	• Library is automated using Integrated Library Management System (ILMS) and has digitisation facility	Yes	3	Physical Verification
	• Adequate facilities of safe and clean drinking water, clean working toilets available in the Library and Departments	Yes	2	Physical Verification & Student Satisfaction Survey
	• Average percentage of expenditure excluding salary for infrastructure augmentation to the total expenditure incurred during the last five years (INR in Lakhs)	>20% 10% - 20% <10%	4 2-3 1	Documentary Evidence
	• Institution has the following Facilities for e-content development (i) Media Centre (ii) Audio Visual Centre (iii) Lecture Capturing System (LCS) (iv) Mixing equipments and software's for editing	Yes	1 1 1 1	Physical Verification

P4.1b	**Availability of Infrastructural Facilities to the Faculty**		**(16)**	
	• Percentage of faculty members provided with dedicated desktops with printers and high-speed internet facility.	>95% 85% - 95% < 85%	4 2-3 1	Physical Verification & Teacher Satisfaction Survey
	• Percentage of faculty members provided with Laptops.	>60% 50% - 60% < 50%	4 2-3 1	
	• Percentage of faculty members provided with separate office chambers.	>95% 85% - 95% < 85%	4 2-3 1	Documentary Evidence & Physical Verification
	• Extent to which faculty member are facilitated with dedicated access to paid data bases to facilitate conduct of research	>95% 85% - 95% < 85%	4 2-3 1	Physical Verification & Teacher Satisfaction Survey
P4.1c	**Facility of Hostel Accommodation**		**(35)**	
	• Percentage of total male applicant students provided hostel accommodation.	>80% 70% - 80% < 70%	4 3-2 1	Physical Verification & Student Survey
	• Percentage of total female applicant students provided hostel accommodation.	>95% 85% - 95% < 85%	4 3-2 1	.....Do....
	• Percentage of male research scholar applicants provided hostel accommodation.	>95% 85% - 95% < 85%	4 3-2 1	.....Do....
	• Percentage of female research scholar applicants provided hostel accommodation.	>95% 85% - 95% < 85%	4 3-2 1	.....Do....
	• Average no. of male and female students accommodated in one room.	2 3 4	5 4 2	.....Do....
	• No. of male and female research scholars accommodated in one room.	1 2 3	5 4 2	.....Do....
	• Affordable accommodation provided to one and all.	Rent Comparable with similar institutions	1	.....Do.... Documentary Evidence
	• Adequate facilities of safe and clean drinking water, clean working toilets, offices, and dining facilities available.	> 95% 85% - 95% < 85%	4 3-2 1	
	• Percentage of Hostels having excess to high-speed internet facility and Wi-Fi.	> 95% 85% - 95% < 85%	4 3-2 1	Physical Verification & Student Survey

P4.1d	**Availability of Medical Facilities**		**(5)**	
	• No. of medical doctors available. • Type of medical facilities available. • No. of ambulances available. • Annual budgetary allocation for medicines, etc.	One for each campus For all emergencies One for each campus 0.025% of non-plan budget	1 1 1 2	Official Records
P4.1e	**Extracurricular Activities:**		**(35)**	
	Facilities for Sports			
	• Percentage of games for which Coaches are available in the university.	>60% 50% - 60% <50%	4 3-2 1	Documentary Evidence
	• Percentage of outdoor games for which playing fields are available.	>80% 70% - 80% <70%	4 3-2 1	Physical Verification
	• University has: ✓ an athletic track and tennis courts. ✓ all weather swimming pool. ✓ boats, tents equipments, etc. for adventure, water sports, trekking and rock climbing. ✓ sufficient and modern health clubs with adequate gym facilities.	 Yes Yes Yes Yes	 1 1 1 1	Physical Verification
	• Percentage of indoor games like, badminton, table tennis, gymnasium, billiards, weightlifting for which playing arenas are available.	>80% 70% - 80% <70%	4 3-2 1	Physical Verification
	Outcome Indicators			
	• Percentage no. of tournaments game-wise organised for male and female students year-wise.	>80% 70% - 80% < 70%	4 3-2 1	Documentary Evidence
	• Percentage no. of inter university tournaments, game-wise organised for male and female students year-wise.	>15% 10% - 15% < 5%	4 3-2 1	Documentary Evidence
	• Percentage no. of tournaments won year-wise.	>25% 25% - 35% <10%	4 3-2 1	Documentary Evidence
	• Percentage no. of students who represented the State or country.	3-5 <2	3-5 2	Documentary Evidence
	• No. of coaching camps organised in association with nationally acclaimed sports-persons per year.	07 - 05 < 5%	2-3 1	Documentary Evidence

P4. 1f	**Extracurricular Activities: Debates, Competitions, Cultural Activities, Literary Activities, etc.**		**(25)**	Documentary Evidence
	• No. of quizzes and debates organised at the:	At least one in each month		
	University Level		1	
	Inter University Level		1	
	State Level		1	Documentary Evidence
	National Level		1	
	• No. of cultural events organised at the:	At least 4 in each year		
	University Level		1	
	Inter University Level		1	Documentary Evidence
	State/National Level		1	
	• No. of music or painting, etc. competitions organised at the:	At least 2 in each year		
	University Level		1	Documentary Evidence
	Inter University Level		1	
	State/National Level		1	
	• No. of quizzes and debates participated by the university at the:	At least one in each year		Documentary Evidence
	Inter University Level		1	
	State level/National Level/ International Level.		1	
	• No. of cultural events participated by the university at the:	At least one in each month		
	Inter University Level		1	Documentary Evidence
	State Level/National Level/ International Level.		1	
	• No. of music or painting, etc. competitions participated by the university at the:	At least 4 in each year		
	Inter University Level		1	Documentary Evidence
	State Level/National Level/ International Level.	At least 2 in each year	1	
	• No. of prizes, medals won by the university in the quizzes, debates, cultural events, music or painting, etc. competitions participated at the:			Documentary Evidence
	University Level	25% - 50%	2-3	
		<25%	1	Documentary Evidence
	Inter University Level	10% - 15%		
		15%	2-3	
	State Level/National Level/		1	
	International Level.	5% - 10%	2-3	
		<5%	1	

Quality Parameter 5: Effective Leadership and Governance (100)

P5	Indicators	Minimum/Maximum Benchmark	Maxi. Score	Validation Process
P5.1a	**Effective Leadership**		(6)	
	• Institution has:			
	• Well defined Vision and Mission	*Yes	1	
	• Has Long-term Strategic Plans	5 years	1	Expert Committee Review
	• Institutional Effectiveness Mechanism	*Yes	1	
	• Frequency of the review of the performance of each Faculty member, Dept., Faculty, student support service centres.	Yearly Basis	1	
	• Has Institutional Strategic Planning Committee	*Yes	1	
	• Has Institutional Effectiveness Committee	*Yes	1	
P5.1b	**Effective Systems of Governance: Human Resources Management Policies and Practices**		(36)	
	• Has Policy of Manpower Planning for:	*Complies with UGC Norms		Expert Committee Review of Policy Documents
	Teaching Staff	* Complies with	1	
	Non-teaching staff	State/UGC Norms	1	
	• Has Policy for the recruitment and appointment of non-teaching staff	Complies with State/UGC Service Rules	1	
	• Has Performance appraisal system for: Non-teaching Staff	*Yes	1	Expert Committee Review of Policy Documents
	• Have Policies for the promotion of: Non-teaching Staff	Complies with State Service/ UGC Rules	1	
	• Has Policy for trainings and development of:			Expert Committee Review of Policy Documents
	Teaching Staff	*Yes	1	
	Non-teaching Staff	*Yes	1	
	• Has Employee grievance redressal mechanism	*Yes	01	Expert Committee Review of Policy Documents
	• Has Policy for Sexual Harassment	*Yes	01	

	Outcome Indicators of Quality HRM Practices			
	• Ratio of non-teach staff to the teaching staff.	<3:1	2	Official Records
		>3:1	1	
	• Ratio of computer literate staff to the total staff.	1:1	2	Official Records
		1:2	1	
	• Average time taken to fill-up vacant positions:			
	(i) Teaching Positions	6 months	1	Official Records &
	(ii) Non-teaching Positions	4 months	1	Staff Survey
	• Percentage of staff positions vacant to the total available sanctioned positions:	<10%	4	Official Records & Staff Survey
	(i) Faculty Positions	10% - 20%	2-3	
		>20%	1	
	(ii) Officers and other staff Positions.	<5%	4	Official Records & Staff Survey
		5% - 15%	2-3	
		>15%	1	Official Records & Staff Survey
	• Percentage of employee grievances to the total employees year-wise.	<5%	4	
		5% - 10%	2-3	
	• Average time taken to redress employees grievances year wise.	<3 weeks	4	Official Records & Staff Survey
		3 - 4 weeks	2-3	
	• No. of sexual harassment cases reported as a percentage of total female employees year-wise.	<1%	3	Official Records & Female Staff Survey
		1% - 5%	2-1	
	• Average time taken to inquire into sexual harassment cases year-wise.	<1 month	2	Official Records & Female Staff Survey
		1 - 2 months	1	
P5.1c	**Financial Management Policies and Practices**		**(33)**	
		UGC Recommended Fund Based	1	
	• Has Scientific Accounting System	Accounting System		Expert Committee Review
	• Has Policy for Financial Reporting	Yes	1	
	• Has Policy for Internal Audit	*Yes	1	Expert Committee
	• Has Policy for Financial Audit of:	*Yes	1	Review
	Funds for Revenue Expenditures, Capital Expenditures, Endowment Funds &Restricted Funds	Independent audit by Chartered Accountant	1	Expert Committee Review
		*Yes		
			1	
	• Policy for Reconciliation of own Revenue funds.	Zero Base Budgeting		Expert Committee Review
			1	
	• Budgeting Practices.			

	Key Indicators of Quality of Financial Management Practices			
	• Frequency of:			
	Reporting of Financial Statements	Annually	1	
	Reporting of Internal Audit Reports	Annually	1	Official Records & Expert Committee Review
	Reporting of Financial Audit Reports	Annually	1	
	Reconciliation of Own Revenue funds	Monthly	1	
	Frequency with which Financial Statements are:			
	Disclosed on the University Website.			Official Records & Expert Committee Review
	Reported to the University Council.	Annually	1	
	• Internal and Financial Audit Reports:			
	Presented before the University Council.	Annually	1	Official Records & Expert Committee Review
	Disclosed on the University Website.			
	• Average Percentage of own revenue sources to the total revenues.	>30% 20% - 30%	3 1-2	Official Records & Expert Committee Review
	• Ratio of annual plan to non-plan expenditures.	>20% 10% - 20%	3 1-2	Official Records & Expert Committee Review
	• Percentage of annual co-curricular & extracurricular expenses to total revenue expenses.	>0.50% 0.25% - 50%	3 1-2	
	• Percentage of annual conferences, seminars, debate and workshop expenses to total revenue expenses.	> 1% 0.75% - 1%	3 1-2	Official Records & Expert Committee Review
	• Percentage of annual Lab expenses to the total revenue expenses.	> 1.5% 0.1% - 1.5%	3 1-2	Official Records & Expert Committee Review

	• Funds/Grants received from government bodies during the last five years for development and maintenance of infrastructure (INR in Crores)	> 150 100 - 150	4 2-3	Official Records & Expert Committee Review
	• Funds/Grants received from non-government bodies, individuals, philanthropists during the last five years for development and maintenance of infrastructure (INR in Crores)	>50 25 - 50	5 3-4	Official Records & Expert Committee Review
P5.1d	**e-governance**		(15)	
	• e-governance is implemented covering following areas of operation: (i) Administration (ii) Finance and Accounts (iii) Student Admission and Support (iv) Examination	Yes	1	Expert Committee Review of E-governance system
	• Status of automation of Examination division along with approved Examination Manual: (i) 100% automation of entire division and implementation of Examination Management System (EMS)	100%	4	
	(ii) Only student registration, Hall ticket issue and Result Processing	100%	3	Expert Committee Review of E-governance system
	(iii) Only student registration and result processing	100%	2	
	(iv) Only result processing	100%	1	

	• Status of IT enabled financial management system:			
	(i) Extent to which Accounting System is Computerised.	100%	3	
	(ii) Extent to which receipt of fee and other dues is online.	100%	2	Expert Committee Review of E-governance system
	(iii) Extent to which payment system is online.	100%	1	
	(iv) Extent to which refund of fee and other dues is online.	100%	1	
	(v) Only manual methodology.		0	
	• Status of IT enabled Admission management system:			Expert Committee Review of E-governance system
	(i) 100% automation of entire admission process.	100%	3	
	(ii) only to the extent to filling of online admission forms and fee.	100%	2	
	(iii) only to the extent of seeking feedback about the Answer Key and	100%	1	
	notifying the merit/ selection list.	100%	1	
	(iv) Only manual methodology.		0	Expert Committee Review of E-governance system
	• Status of automation of administration division along with approved Administrative Manual			
	(i) 100% automation of entire work from the point of online submission to the approval or otherwise.	100%	3	
	(ii) Only online submission of different forms for seeking necessary certificates.	100%	1	
	(iii) Only manual methodology.	100% 100%	0	Official Records
	• Online student grievance redressal system	Yes	1	

P5.1e	**Participative Decision-making**		**(10)**	
	• Frequency with which following apex decision-making bodies met: University Council University Syndicate Finance Committee Academic Council	Twice a year Twice a year Twice a year Twice a year	2	Minutes of the meetings
	• Statutory Committees constituted and met to transact business as per the university Act/Statutes	*Yes	1	
	• Non-statutory committees constituted and met to transact the business as per the terms and references of the committees.	*Yes	1	Documentary Evidence and Minutes of the meetings
	• Faculty members, non-teaching staff, students, scholars, nominees of different employee bodies/ Associations and alumni allowed to participate in decision-making.	*Yes	1	Documentary Evidence and Minutes of the meetings
	• To allow easy access to the information pertaining to different aspects of governance, have the following policy documents circulated among all the concerned: (i) Recruitment and promotion policies/rules. (ii) Service rules. (iii) Accounting policy. (iv) Internal Audit policy. (v) Library policy. (vi) Admission policy. (vii) Assessment and Grade appeal policy. (viii) Research policy. (ix) Hostel accommodation and residence policy. (x) Policy for Anti Plagiarism. (xi) Fire Safety Policy. (xii) Policy for sexual harassment redressal.	*Yes	5	Documentary Evidence & Expert Committee Review

Quality Parameter 6: Social Responsibility and Distinctiveness (50)

P6	Indicators	Minimum/ Maximum Benchmark	Maxi. Score	Validation Process
P6.1a	**Community Engagement and Service**		**(25)**	
	• No. of programmes organised to educate and aware the students about the issues like: (i) Climate Change, (ii) Pollution Control, (iii) Waste management, (iv) Sanitation, (v) Forest and wildlife conservation, energy conservation of energy.	At least one programme each month on each of these issues	3	Expert Committee Review of Documentary Evidence
	• No. of programmes organised to educate and aware the society at large about the issues like: (i) Climate change, (ii) Pollution Control, (iii) Waste management, (iv) Sanitation, (v) Forest and wildlife conservation. Conservation of Energy.	At least one programme each month on each of these issues	3	Expert Committee Review of Documentary Evidence
	• No. of extension activities in the neighbourhood community in terms of impact and sensitising students about social issues and for their holistic development during the last five years.	At least one activity each month	3	Expert Committee Review of Documentary Evidence
	• Number of awards received by the Institution, its teachers and students from Government/ Government recognised bodies in recognition of the extension activities carried out during the last five years.	>5	3	Expert Committee Review of Documentary Evidence

	• Number of extension and outreach programmes conducted by the institution including those through NSS/NCC/Red cross/YRC during the last five years (including Government initiated programmes such as Swachh Bharat, Aids Awareness, Gender Issue, etc. and those organised in collaboration with industry, community and NGOs)	At least one programme each month	5	Expert Committee Review of Documentary Evidence
	• Specific facilities provided for women in terms of: (i) Safety and security (ii) Counselling (iii) Common Rooms (iv) Day care centre for young children (v) Any other relevant information.	Yes	5	Physical Verification & Female staff Survey
	• Sensitization of students and employees of the Institution to the constitutional obligations: values, rights, duties and responsibilities of citizens	At least six programme each year	3	Expert Committee Review of Documentary Evidence
P6.1b	**Environmental Education, and Value-Based Education**		**(8)**	
	• Provision in the curriculum for value-based education aiming to build character so as to enable learners to be ethical.	>5% of the total courses relate to value based education	3	Expert Committee Review of Course curriculum
	• Institution celebrates/organizes national and international commemorative days, events and festivals.	Yes	3	Expert Committee Review of Documentary Evidence
	• Number of value-added courses for imparting transferable and life skills offered during the last five years.	>7% of the total courses offered	2	Expert Committee Review of Course Curriculum

P6.1c	**Equity and Access to Education**		**(8)**	
	• Has provision of financial assistance and scholarships to socio-economically disadvantaged students.	50% concession in admission fee	3	Official Records
	• Has admissions processes which is more inclusive.	Complies with national reservation policy	1	Expert Committee Review of Admission Process
	• Has provision of bridge courses for students coming from disadvantaged educational backgrounds.	*Yes	1	Expert Committee Review of Course Curriculum
	• Provide socio-emotional and academic support and mentoring to all such students through suitable counselling and mentoring programmes.	*Yes	1	Expert Committee Review
	• Percentage of students belonging to socio-economically disadvantaged classes of the society admitted to the total students.	> 5%	2	Admission Records
P6.1d	**Conservation of Natural Resources and Ecology**		**(9)**	
	• The Institution has facilities for alternate sources of energy and energy conservation:			
	(i) Solar energy	Yes	1	Physical Assessment
	(ii) Biogas plant	Yes	1	
	(iii) Wheeling to the Grid	Yes	1	
	(v) Use of LED bulbs/power efficient equipment	Yes	1	
	• Measures taken by the university for: Rain Water harvesting. Waste recycling. Carbon neutral and green practices..	Yes	1	Physical Assessment
	• Use of Bicycles/Battery powered vehicles	Yes	1	
	• Ban on use of Plastic	Yes	1	
	• Green Initiatives (Landscaping with trees and plants)	Yes	1	
		Yes	1	

Index

A

Academic, 8, 22, 32, 43, 46-48, 58, 80, 88-89, 93, 102, 106, 123, 128, 141, 169

Academicians, 35, 44-45, 60, 62, 68, 70-71, 80-84, 87-91, 97

Accounting policy, 138, 169

Administration, 97, 103, 108-09, 126, 138, 167-68

Administrative, 4, 35, 42-44, 46, 70-71, 80-85, 88-90, 93, 132, 153

Anti Plagiarism, 139, 169

Artificial intelligence, 5, 12, 33, 67, 74, 132

Aspirations, 84, 94, 99, 106

Autonomy, 3-5, 10, 14, 29, 33, 35, 43-48, 55-58, 83, 92-93, 96, 113-14, 118, 128, 137, 143

B

Bachelor's degree, 11-13, 20, 35, 39-41, 51, 53

Brain Drain, 29, 35, 61-65

C

Character, 49, 86, 93, 139, 171

College, 4, 33, 38, 40, 112, 132

Communication, 38, 46, 109-10, 114

Community development, 55, 92-93, 123, 131

Companies, 144

Conferences, 134, 138, 158-59, 166

Counselling, 42, 149, 171

COVID, 73

Customers of HEIs, 123

D

Destination, 94

Devotion, 44-45, 59, 70, 79, 90, 97

Discipline Core, 38-40

E

Ecosystem, 123, 131, 152

Effective Leadership, 123, 136, 164

E-governance, 137, 167, 168

Employability, 144

Environment, 3, 10, 12, 14, 58, 93, 95, 100, 104, 106, 113, 118, 121, 130, 131, 134

Environment education, 10

Evaluation, 29, 73, 77, 100, 103, 106-07, 112, 131

F

Feedback, 104

Financial assistance, 25-26, 139, 172

Foreign universities, 9, 62

Fundamental principles, 54

G

Galvanise, 85, 90, 97

Gender, 25-26, 107, 112, 171

General Education Council, 7

Governance, 4, 9, 54, 60, 70, 79-80, 84, 92-96, 100-01, 104, 107, 136-38, 167-69

Government of India, 3, 18, 24, 31, 64

Gross Enrolment Ratio, 17

H

HEIs, 4-5, 7-8, 11, 13-15, 17, 20, 25, 27, 32-38, 41-43, 48, 52, 53, 58, 63, 84, 99, 100-02, 104, 108, 121-24, 128, 130, 139

Higher education, 3, 6-8, 10, 12-15, 17-18, 20, 25-27, 31-32, 34, 36-37, 42, 48-49, 50-52, 61, 64, 67, 72-73, 76, 113, 121, 123-24, 127, 132, 151

Higher Education Grants Council, 7

Higher education policy, 3

Honesty, 70, 82, 90, 96-97

I

Indian Council for Agricultural Research, 7

Industry, 5, 11-13, 41, 51-53, 69, 133, 152, 155-56, 171

Infrastructural, 15, 27, 36, 46, 56, 106, 136

Institutions, 6-8, 19, 43, 79, 121, 124-25, 145

Integrity, 19, 45, 57, 59, 65, 71, 74, 79-80, 82-83, 86, 88, 90, 93, 95, 97, 118, 124, 127

Intellectual, 60, 70, 82, 95, 153

International students, 8-9, 34-35, 62-63

Internet, 75, 117, 134-35, 159, 161

K

Knowledge, 19, 55, 91

Kothari Commission, 49

L

Leadership crisis, 60, 84

Leadership Qualities, 77, 88, 92

Learning, 3-5, 7, 10-12, 14, 16, 26, 33, 41, 47, 49, 55, 57-58, 67, 74-76, 79, 84, 93, 96, 106-08, 111, 113-16, 118, 129-32, 137, 139, 147-49

Likert, 103, 109, 110

M

Mechanism, 95, 101-02, 104, 106, 130, 136-37, 149, 164

Merit, 95, 129, 145-46

Multidisciplinary education, 3, 8, 10, 12, 34, 36, 38

N

National Accreditation Council, 7

National Higher Education Regulatory Council, 4, 6

National Research Foundation, 5, 33, 68

National Testing Agency, 21

NEP, 25, 31-32, 35, 38, 50-51, 57-58, 62-64, 68, 79, 84, 101, 114, 118, 121, 124, 127, 140

NET, 56, 131, 150

Nobel Prize, 70

O

Online admission, 138, 168

Online teaching, 74-76

Open Distance Learning, 14

P

Panacea, 77, 99

Pedagogy, 14, 147

Personal Integrity, 90, 96-97

Policy, 3-6, 8, 10, -22, 24-28, 31-44, 46-48, 51, 54, 56-61, 63-64, 69-72, 82, 84, 89, 91, 113, 118, 131-33, 137-39, 150, 153, 155, 169, 172

Policymakers, 6, 41

Poverty, 5, 23-24, 67

Public policy, 60, 69-70, 133

Q

Quality Assurance, 100, 119, 121

Quality Parameters, 119, 127, 141

Quality research, 5, 33, 35, 56, 68-69, 71, 132, 153

R

Registrar, 89

S

Scholarships, 7, 20-21, 25-26, 130, 139, 150, 172

Search Committee, 85-86

Secondary school, 13, 42, 49, 51

Seminars, 134, 138, 153, 158-59, 166

Skill courses, 51-53

Skill Development, 50, 144

Skill Mapping, 52

Society, 24, 27, 58-59, 63-64, 67, 69, 70, 75, 106, 123, 133, 139, 155, 170-72

Special Education Zones, 25, 27

Steve Jobs, 96

Strategic Plan, 101-02, 136

Synergy, 6, 95-96, 137

T

Teacher education, 3, 10, 18-21, 113

Teacher Education Institutes (TEIs), 21

Teamwork, 93, 96, 118, 137
Technical education, 12
Technology, 8, 12, 14, 16, 26, 38, 64, 67, 70, 75, 93, 123, 130-35, 148, 154, 159
Territory sectors, 49
Tournaments, 135-36, 162
Traditional vocations, 53

U

UGC, 6, 22, 51, 69, 80, 82, 85, 88, 121, 146, 156, 164-65
Undergraduate, 4-5, 11-12, 20, 33, 38, 40, 51, 116
Undergraduate Education, 10
United Nations, 24
University, 4-5, 15-16, 22, 33, 42, 44-47, 49, 59, 68, 71, 79, 81, 85, 87, 89-90, 92-95, 97, 100-02, 115, 133-36, 142-45, 158, 162-63, 169, 172

V

Value-based education, 10, 139, 171
Veterinary Council of India, 7
Visionary, 79, 85, 90, 94, 97
Vocational education, 3, 7, 10, 12-13, 17, 20, 34, 49, 50-51, 53-54, 113

W

Western World, 70
Workshops, 129, 134, 147, 153, 158

Y

Yash Pal Committee Report, 88
Yoga, 8, 62